THE LUATH GUIDES

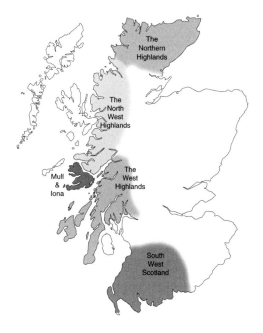

The Northern Highlands

The North West Highlands

Mull & Iona

The West Highlands

South West Scotland

South West Scotland
The West Highlands: the Lonely Lands
Mull & Iona: Highways & Byways
The North West Highlands: Roads to the Isles
The Northern Highlands: the Empty Lands

The Northern Highlands:
The Empty Lands

TOM ATKINSON

Luath Press Limited

EDINBURGH

www.luath.co.uk

First Edition 1986
Second Impression 1986
Second Edition 1987
Third Edition 1988
Revised Edition 1989
Revised and Enlarged Edition 1991
New Edition 1992
New Edition 1993
Revised Edition 1994
Revised Edition 1995
Revised Edition 1997
Revised Edition 1999

The paper used in this book is acid-free, neutral-sized and recyclable.
It is made from low chlorine pulps produced in a low energy,
low emission manner from sustainable forests.

Printed and bound by
Bell & Bain Ltd., Glasgow

Typeset in 10.5 point Sabon by
S. Fairgrieve, Edinburgh, 0131 658 1763

A message from the Publishers

Our authors welcome feedback from their readers, so do please let us have your comments and suggestions. The feedback we have received indicates that the Luath Guides are valued by their readers and that their usefulness is enhanced by the inclusion of advertisements for local businesses whose support Luath Press greatly appreciates. We, in turn, encourage our readers to make use of their products and services. Mention Luath Press when you do. The author's editorial independence is unaffected by the inclusion of these advertisements.

Whilst we make every effort to ensure that information in our books is correct, we can accept no responsibility for any accident, loss or inconvenience arising.

SUILEAN

Togaibh ur suilean;
chi sibh boidhchead nam beann,
loch fada, cuan air faire, eilean.
Ca bheil boidhchead mur eil suilean ann?

Dh'fhalbh na suilean gu preidhridhean,
beanntan eile, eileanan fad as,
tur-taighean's na bailtean-mora.

Is co iad, an fheadainn air a'mhointich?

Thanaig iad, nuair a dh'fhalbh suilean dhaoine,
suilean nan eun a dhunadh,
gloinne a chur an aite suilean chabrach
is doille bais an aite suilean gaoil.

Togaibh ur suilean, ma tha, chum nam beann.

Uilleam Neill

EYES

Lift up your eyes;
you will see the beauty of the mountains,
long loch, sea on horizon, island.
Where is beauty if there are no eyes?

The eyes left for prairies,
other mountains, islands afar off,
tower-blocks in the cities.

And who are they, those on the moor?

They came after the eyes of men had left
to close the eyes of the birds,
to put glass in place of the stags' eyes
and the blindness of death in place of the eyes of love.

Lift up your eyes, then, to the hills.

William Neill

A Note On Spelling

The correct spelling of Gaelic is still a matter of argument amongst those who care. Gaelic is an oral, rather than a written language, and its orthography is by no means settled. Throughout this book, the many Gaelic names have been spelled according to the system followed by the cartographers of John Bartholomew of Edinburgh. Not everyone will agree with every spelling, but at least let them recognise that an effort has been made.

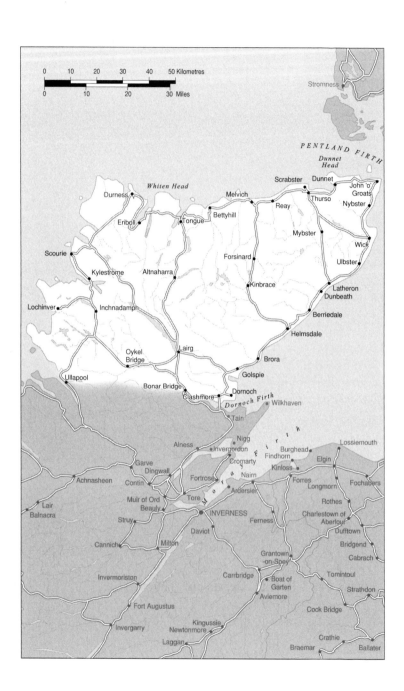

Contents

Foreword

Royal Mail is committed to providing mail services to communities throughout Scotland.

As part of our commitment to rural communities, Royal Mail runs a network of postbus services – mail vehicles which carry passengers as well as mail and provide a valuable service in areas where no other public transport exists. These services are used both by local people and by tourists travelling throughout Scotland. Postbus timetables are available from local tourist offices.

In this, the National Year of Reading in Scotland, Royal Mail is delighted to support this series of Luath Guides written by people who have a thorough knowledge of the area and an enthusiasm to share a love of Scotland with their readers.

Please enjoy reading them as you travel around Scotland.

Alex Gibb

Alex Gibb
Director and General Manager
Royal Mail Scotland & Northern Ireland

Introduction

WHY THE EMPTY LANDS? Why not *A Guide to Wester Ross and Sutherland?* Or *Highland Delights* or some such title? I may say that choosing a title for a book is by no means the easiest part of writing it. And then the marketing people have their say. Is it eye-catching? Will it sell? When the marketing manager happens to be married to the author, as in my case, such discussions can go on all day – then all night.

To me, a book title must be both evocative and true, and so far as possible, encapsulate the whole book. This is so with *The Empty Lands*, for the area covered by this book is indeed empty. Of course, there are towns and villages by the score, but the essence of Scotland's far north and west is its emptiness. Emptiness of people, that is, but of nothing else that brings delight to any tired soul. As a matter of fact, a better title would have been *The Emptied Lands*, but that is trying to fit too much into a small measure.

Mountains and moors, lochs and lochans, burns and cliffs, beaches and islands – northern Scotland has them all, and has them in a plenty that seems prodigal. But the people have gone, leaving that emptiness which today we love, but in which love is tinged always with a sadness that seems inseparable from the soul of the Gael.

In this book you will find much of the Clearances, for an understanding of that episode in Scottish history is a vital foundation for better appreciating what delights you today. There is bitterness, and little effort to disguise it, and why should there be? But I have also tried to convey something of the sheer magic of the Highlands, something of the joy that comes from such a

Land of the Mountain and the Flood

cornucopia of loveliness, for the Highlands are lovely beyond words.

This is an ancient country, and its beauty comes from age. The land has been planed and honed by glaciers and by water and wind over many centuries. It has suffered wars and invasions and clan battles beyond number. Its few natural resources have been plundered again and again – that is still happening and the only one who has not grown rich from the Highlands is the Highlander. Here are some of the oldest mountains in the world, once higher than those young upstarts the Alps.

Perhaps because these mountains are so old, there is a strange, and even weird quality about them, something unexpected. There is also a strange violence in the contrast between the stark barrenness of the harsh scree slopes, the great sea-scourged cliffs and the quiet secret places, sweet and serene, with gentle clear streams running through green valleys, and idyllic bays where a wonderfully translucent sea swells green above white or red sand. The Highlands are a succession of natural dramas, some comic, most tragic.

It is of course a land of warriors, and whenever warriors are needed the Highlander is cherished. Then he goes back to be forgotten and derided and exploited until the next time he is needed.

But who, and what, is the Highlander? Perhaps no other group of people in these islands has been so romanticised and caricatured. Sir Walter Scott, whose romantic and misty ideas of Scottish history still distort understanding, depicted them as fierce warriors, bearded and tartan-clad, and with a fervent, unthinking loyalty to clan and principles. These were the Rob Roys, and although of course they existed, they surely were not the norm. The massacre of Culloden and the appalling genocide which followed ended whatever truth there had ever been in that caricature.

George IV, ludicrous and be-tartaned, and with the

assistance again of Sir Walter Scott, resurrected the Highlander, but this time as another myth. That new myth was perpetuated by Queen Victoria, whose infatuation with all things Highland knew neither bounds nor propriety. She was responsible for the 'Highland Gathering Highlander' and for what followed, the funny-postcard Highlander.

The Scots themselves are quite capable of caricaturing their own, and it was Harry Lauder who created the whisky-swilling Highlander. All of these caricatures, like all caricatures, have a touch of truth in them, and yet every one is as untrue as the Welsh Taffy, the Irish Paddy and the English Hodge.

In fact, the Highlander of today is little different from the rest of the people in these islands, but what differences there are have been forged over the centuries of a tragic history. Perhaps it is in having memories of such a history that the Highlander differs most.

This is a time of transition, just possibly of recovery, for the Highlands and the Highlanders, after having gone through a period of travail such as few other people have endured, and certainly none in these islands.

Today we cannot define the Highlander solely in terms of language, for that language has suffered a long eclipse, one which might be passing, but which still casts the deepest of shadows. The language was Gaelic, a Celtic language, and thus the people could be called Gaels. The Gaels first appeared out of the mists of history in 498 AD, when they came to what is now Argyll from what is now Ireland. Why they came is by no means sure, but perhaps it was simply because it was new land to be colonised, new horizons to survey, for there is no reason to suppose that the spirit of adventure is a modern phenomenon.

Although Scotland was by no means empty of people when the Gaels arrived, those who inhabited the land could not withstand (and maybe they did not even try) the superior organisation and culture of the Gaels, who rapidly spread over the whole country.

Centuries later, the Anglo-Saxon language, the precursor of English, took root in the south, and a cultural division appeared, one which still plagues the country. The Gaels became isolated, but their society was still strong, still organised in families or 'clans', and with their own rulers, who were often powerful rivals to the Kings of Scotland, who had become feudal or at least semi-feudal in their ideas of statehood.

As rulers always do, the Kings sought to exert their control by a policy of divide and rule. It was this which led to so much of the blood-shed in the Highlands, as the kings favoured first one clan then another, and encouraged the favourite of today to eliminate the favourite of yesterday.

During many centuries, the Crown of England sought to rule Scotland, and warfare between the two States was almost incessant. It was under the blows of Edward I of England, 'The Hammer of the Scots', that Scotland was forged into a nation-state led by Robert Bruce.

In 1320 the remarkable Declaration of Arbroath was written, a document in which all the nobles of Scotland expressed their ideals:

> So long as a hundred of us remain alive, we shall never, under any conditions, submit to English domination. It is not for glory, riches, nor honours that we fight, but for Liberty alone, which no good man gives up except with his life...

That national unity did not long endure, for to a large extent it was based on the strength and personality of Bruce. With his death it began to crumble, and the division between the Highlands and the rest of the country was found to be as deep as ever. The clans began, or in some cases resumed, the practice of rivalries and feuds, suspicion and fear, bloodshed and warfare, with each chief and chieftain seeking power and wealth at the expense of his neighbours.

That is the reality behind the misty romanticism of Highland history – it is a blood-stained record of petty rivalries and major horrors, with the chiefs intent on ensuring that no breath of modernity crept into their fiefdoms, where the value of a chief was measured not by wealth and culture but by the number and ferocity of his fighting men.

It was not a time of romance and Arcadian delight. It was a time of torment, and the clan chiefs were perhaps the most bloodthirsty, evil and grasping ruling clique in all of European history.

Of course, life went on for the common people. They lived in a system of mutual support in a close community, bound together by ties of blood or loyalty to the chief. They had rights to their land, and they farmed. Their wealth was in animals: cattle, goats, sheep and horses. There were crops to be grown, fish to be caught and game to be hunted. There was a strong culture, and that culture is almost all that now remains, in a very emaciated form, to distinguish the Highlanders of today. Story-telling, poetry, songs, pipe and harp music – that was a powerful cement, and it bound together chief and clansmen. Certainly the old Highlander was illiterate, but was well educated in an oral culture and his own history.

So, in essence, what identified the Highlander of old was a language, a culture, a history and a society. In fact, just about everything except a different blood strain!

As it transpired, the one thing that finally shattered the old social contract in the Highlands, and thus most affected the Highlander, was something that is much more difficult to identify, but what was in effect no more than patriotism – Jacobitism, or faith to the Stuart line of kings. This was no simple romantic longing, but a complex of political, economic, social and even religious aspirations. The most important constituent of that complexity was probably the desire to have a state and nation of Scotland again, for Scotland had been swallowed up in the Union, first of Crowns, and then of Parliaments, and was increasingly being treated as no more than a province, even a colony, of England.

Three times in thirty years the Jacobites rose in arms against the English crown, and three times they went down to defeat. Finally, after the 1745 Rising, led by the gallant, romantic, stupid, pig-headed Prince Charles Edward, Bonny Prince Charlie of the picture books, the English had had enough, and embarked on a passage of genocidal revenge that left the Highlands a desert and the Highlanders shattered, scattered and demoralised.

The Highlander was forbidden his dress, his language, his music, his arms and his chiefs. It was a series of devastating blows from which the Highlands has never recovered.

The travail began immediately the Jacobite Army had been shattered by the English artillery at Culloden. The order was that the wounded were to be killed, and they were, being bayonetted as they lay bleeding. The countryside, all that great richness of glen and strath with its wealth of houses and animals, was pillaged, the houses burned, the cattle hamstrung or driven off, the women raped. The clan system was destroyed and all over the Highlands a terrible act of genocidal revenge was enacted. The beheading axe, the hanging rope and the disembowelling knife were kept busy, and many hundreds of families were sold off to slavery in the plantations of America.

But Bonny Prince Charlie was awa', safely o'er the bounding main, off to Rome where he lived another forty years, brandy-bloated and brutal to his wife, and seemed never to give a thought to the hardship of those whose love and loyalty he had so exploited.

But the worst blow was the suborning of the Highland chiefs who were taught to crave for the only things the Highlands could not supply, but which wealth could buy in London. Big houses, fancy clothes and fancier women, the excitement of the card table, the ostentation of wealth. Out they came from their Highland fastnesses, the chiefs of their clans, to be feted and fawned over, and they needed money, not a 'tail' of fighting men.

Rents were screwed up on the clan lands, lands which the English law now declared to belong to the chiefs, but that hardly proved enough. They wanted gold, lots of it and quickly. So estates were sold to newly-rich English manufacturers and Lowland sheep farmers, and the hell of the Clearances began, when the tenant farmers of the Highlands were ruthlessly driven off the land they had farmed down the centuries, to make room for sheep.

It was a time of horror and degradation so intense that it far surpassed anything that had gone before in sad Highland history. It was a diaspora that scattered the Highlanders to the far corners of the world and into the stinking slums of every city in England and Scotland. It was a time of toil that has never been forgotten, and never will be.

And what made it worse was that the Highlanders had never expected anything but patriarchal protection from their clan chiefs (with occasional rough justice, but that was accepted), but now their chiefs had sold out, and did not hear the cries from the glens. It was a betrayal, and a sad one, but the Judas-chiefs had their gold, and departed.

The 18th and 19th centuries were a period of horror for the Highlanders, with the loss of Scottish nationality, and the Scottish state, the Jacobite uprisings, the genocide after Culloden, the Clearances and the potato famines. It left a poor remnant of a once proud people sad and isolated, seeking relief in a strict religion, looking for acceptance in a political union which had no use for their culture, their language, their heritage, or anything about them except their numbers when the war drums thundered. They grew to despise their own language, to see themselves as fit only to be gillies (a contemptuous term which means only 'boy') or servants in the Big House. The Highlander even forgot what had been lost.

Well, things are changing. Today the Highlander is slowly re-asserting a language, a culture and a history that have much to offer. Only time will tell whether the sickness of the past and the wounds (so many of them self-inflicted) can be healed, and the Highlander again stand proud as the representative of a noble past and a promising future.

Just the same, how can a visitor identify a Highlander? Certainly not because he wears a kilt or carries bagpipes. You will see more kilts in London than in Lairg; more kilts swing above the knobbly knees of English hotel keepers in the Highlands than on the stout hurdies of the Highlanders themselves.

You can learn something from names, of course, for any 'Mac' is of the old Gaelic stock. But then, so are Campbells, Camerons, Grants, Frasers and many more.

It really comes down to language, and that language is Gaelic, which truly identifies the Gael. Not all Highlanders speak Gaelic, and today, delightfully, not all Gaelic speakers have Highland ancestry. (There is a strong colony of immigrants from the Indian sub-continent in the Hebrides, and they are Gaelic speakers.) I would argue that those of Highland ancestry, wherever they live, who reject their language are not Highland, and that all, whatever their ancestry, who speak or even respect Gaelic, are at least honorary Highlanders. So what is this language? Is it truly, as the Gaels say, the language spoken in Eden? Well, hardly, but it is an ancient tongue and a flexible one. It is a language perfectly well fitted for contemporary use, and with a wealth of song and poetry perhaps unsurpassed in Europe, although those who speak its sister tongue, Welsh, would contest that. It is a language that a thousand years ago was the only language of Scotland; since then it has gradually retreated under the strange linguistic imperialism of English to find a haven in the Highlands and Islands.

Poetry and song have from time immemorial been precious to the Gael, and a very important member of every clan and chief's household was the Bard. It was not only his task to sing the praises of the clan and its chief, but also to act as the repository of history. He also made poetry about the everyday things of life, the hunts, the weather, the scenery, and love:

Farewell for Anna to last night.
Swift though it passed, its joy remains.
Though I were hanged for my share in it, I'd live it over again tonight.
There are two in this house tonight
whose eyes give their secrets away:
though they are not lip to lip, eager is the eyes' play.
The eyes' swift glances must give all the tale that pressed lips would tell;
the eyes have kept no secret here;
lips silenced to no avail.

Those who would make my true words false,
have sealed my lips, oh languid eyes.
But in your corner, out of reach,
understand what our eyes say:
'Keep the memory of this night,
let there be no change till dawn;
do not let the morning in:
throw out the cold day from the room.'
Mother Mary, fostering grace, since spirits look to you for light,
Save me now, and take my hand – farewell for ever to last night.

What could be more lovely than that evocation of passion partially quenched? And yet it was made by a *Fili*, one of the hereditary poets, almost a thousand years ago, and is still as fresh as tomorrow's dawning. It was composed in Gaelic, a despised language for which, only fifty years ago, children were beaten for using in the school playground, as though it was some filthy argot of criminals and perverts.

Of course, there is more to Highland culture than poems of aching beauty. There is music, and essentially that is the music of the bagpipe, the *pieb-mhor* (great pipe). There is the clarsach, the Gaelic harp, and the fiddle, and today the ubiquitous 'box' (accordion) and guitar. Of them all, it is the pipes and the clarsach which are indigenous to the Highlands.

That is not to say that either of them originated there, for both harp and bagpipes are found world wide, and both are very ancient indeed. One version of the Book of Genesis has the Hebrews playing bagpipes, so perhaps it is not altogether too far-fetched to hold that Gaelic was indeed the language of Eden!

Everyone is familiar with the bagpipes today, and surely everyone has been stirred by the sight of a military pipe band in full regalia, marching and counter-marching, kilts swinging, with a pipe major at least 10 feet tall – there can be no more colourful sight. We are all familiar, too, with many a pipe tune, not least Amazing Grace.

However, there is another sort of pipe music, and it differs from the military version as much as a pop song differs from a Bach Fugue, and it is no stretch of reality to compare the *Piobaireachd* (Pibroch) to Bach. Listen to a pibroch, a real one, played by a master piper, and you will hear a range of composition and an execution quite remarkable. It begins with the *Urlar* or theme, and then goes off into a complexity of variations, each following a traditional pattern and each demanding a fingering skill, a breath control and a profundity of musical feeling and understanding. Listen to the great

MacCrimmon's *Lament for the Only Son*, and you will hear musical composition and skill of an order certainly comparable to Bach's Requiem. Listen to *MacIntosh's Lament*, and you will learn where Dvorak got his inspiration for his New World Symphony, and yet the Lament dates back to the first years of the 16th century.

The bagpipe is a truly Highland instrument, part of the heritage of Highland culture, but a part which has spread across the world, and yet is still associated with the north of Scotland, a strange, long-lost, almost outrageously beautiful part of the world.

This book presents many problems, not the least of which is the dearth of superlatives in the English language. When you have spoken of 'the magnificent grandeur' of a view, how do you describe what waits around the corner, even more magnificent and even grander? That is a real problem in writing about the Highlands, where virtually everything is magnificent and grand. And having done so, has the essence of the Highlands still escaped me?

I do not believe it worthwhile simply to visit and admire, and yet understand nothing of what has created the object of admiration. To look at a Highland glen, empty and lovely, and not realise that once, not long ago, it was vibrant with the life of a healthy community, is to me pointless. So there is history in this book and legend, and perhaps a good deal of lecturing and certainly a great deal of bitterness for what happened in the past and fear for what might happen in the future.

And even so, I fear that I have not done what I sought to do. I have tried to make the complex simple, the beautiful accessible and the strange familiar. I trust that I have succeeded to the extent that the visitor will leave with some understanding of and sympathy with the Highlands, as well as with a great awe at the sheer beauty of it all.

There is much more that could be said. One of the greatest

factors of change has been the electrification of the Highlands, a scheme of high vision and considerable success, that has brought electricity to every glen and loch-side in the Highlands, and has proved to be both a revolutionary and a destructive force.

It is more than sixty years ago that Lenin realised that electrification was revolutionary, and he was right. The introduction of a new source of power into what is essentially a peasant community opens up the possibility, even the likelihood, of social and economic change. It has happened in the Highlands, where now, for the first time, the Highlander can live, and even prosper in a mild way, without the constant and backbreaking toil of the past. It is a destructive force, too, of course, thanks largely to television, with its seductive visions of a way of life and an implied pattern of ideals totally foreign to the Highlanders. Today, sadly, the TV has largely replaced the ceilidh, and the greatest influence on the young is no longer the storytellers round the peat fire but the voice from the box beside the artificial coals of 'the electric'.

The North of Scotland Hydro Electricity Board was one of the great successes of State enterprise. The Board has a motto: *Neart nan Gleann* – Strength of the Glens – and it is fitting. It all began with the vision of Tom Johnston, Secretary of State for Scotland during the last war. Tom Johnston was much more than that, though. He was a journalist, historian, socialist, member of Parliament, Privy Councillor, and finally Companion of Honour. A great man indeed, a man both of ideas and action, and a man of ideals. In his vision, Tom Johnston saw that the provision of electricity to the Highlands and Islands would provide a great opportunity to improve both social and economic conditions in an area that was at least economically backward, and certainly ignored.

He was impressed by the great Tennessee Valley Authority in America, and in the Parliamentary Bill setting up the Hydro

Board, he insisted that it must be much more than an organisation to generate and distribute electricity. The Bill stated that the new Board would: '...so far as their powers and duties permit, collaborate in carrying out any measure for the economic and social improvements of the North of Scotland or any part thereof.'

When the various private electricity boards were nationalised in 1948, the Hydro covered 26,000 sq. miles, two-thirds of the area of Scotland, one-quarter of the whole UK, but with only 2% of the population of the UK. In its major period of expansion, between 1945 and 1965, the Hydro employed as many as 12,000 workers on construction programmes, and it permanently changed the face of the Highlands. Many lochs were dammed and their power was harnessed. Generating stations were built, many of them in very remote places; new roads were cut, and the country enmeshed in power lines. It was all done with proper regard to the environment, even though that word had hardly been invented then, and all the necessary buildings were appropriately designed, and with considerable grace. It was a splendid effort, and it still continues.

As a result of all the activity, about 16,000 new jobs were created, and thirty three new industries established. Without doubt the Hydro Board has changed the face of the Highlands and has offered the Highlander a new way forward. Whether it will be taken is still uncertain.

These, then, are the Empty Lands, the far north of Scotland. Visit it and enjoy it, for it is a land of endless natural beauty. But with your enjoyment mingle a little sadness for a sorrowful past.

Tom Atkinson

CHAPTER I

Ullapool

ULLAPOOL IS A PLANNED VILLAGE. It did not just grow, Topsy-like, by chance, but was built and planned as a whole by the British Fisheries Society in 1788. Herring was the attraction; they shoaled in untold millions in Loch Broom and the adjacent waters. There had been much fishing here long before the Fisheries Society established itself, and there are traces of old curing stations here and there. But the Society brought big capital that was invested in a pier, storehouses, an inn and fishermen's houses.

There is a fascinating report in the *First Statistical Account of Scotland* of what happened when the herring shoals appeared:

> People are instantly afloat with every species of sea-worthy craft... They press forward with utmost eagerness to the field of slaughter – sloops, schooners, wherries, boats of all sizes, are to be seen constantly flying on the wings of the wind from creek to creek and from loch to loch, according as the varying reports of men, of the noisy flights of birds, or tumbling and spouting of whales and porpoises attract them...

It was too good to last, of course, and the herring were fished out after half a century. By the second half of the last century, Ullapool had gone into a deep depression, its very reason for existing having vanished.

But it is booming again today, and again with fishing, for improved boats and gear allow herring to be fished in other waters, far away, and there are also the great migrant shoals of mackerel to be exploited – for how long, no-one can predict, for there is as little thought of conservation now as in the 18th century.

The major ferry for Lewis now runs from Ullapool twice daily, and that adds much to the bustle of the town. From here you can also join the intricate network of MacBrayne's ferries that knit the islands together. Surely there can be few more satisfying ways of spending a holiday than island-hopping through the Hebrides.

Ullapool is certainly a busy place, but equally certainly it has not succumbed to the temptation of adopting the lowest common denominator of tourist traps. It is busy because it is a working port, and everything is subordinated to that. But it is an attractive town, well situated and organised.

For the visitor, there is much here. Sea-angling, especially, is a great attraction, and it is so good that several international competitions have been held. You can fish from the shore or from a boat, and if you are particularly ambitious, there is game fishing for the big ones, including shark.

There is not much of a beach at Ullapool – it is all shingle – but just north a mile or so at Ardmair there is a splendid beach, made all the more attractive by its backdrop of the great cliffs of Coigach towering up 2,500 feet. Ardmair is also a place for collecting semi-precious stones from the beach. They are not always easy to recognise in their raw state (wet any possibles to check their colour), but amethysts, quartz of many kinds, cornelians and moss agates are quite common.

As for walking, you really can't do better than follow the tiny road up the Ullapool river and up Glen Achall, past Loch Achall and away into the hills. Where the road ends, a track begins, and you can follow that eastwards, if you will, all the way to distant Oykel Bridge on the A837. It is wild and lonely country, through the Rhidorroch Forest and Glen Einig, but it is walking of rare grandeur.

There is a small museum at Ullapool, tucked away behind a bookshop. This is another community project, and it contains items of both local and general interest. It is a crammed little place, and some of the exhibits are rather bizarre, but are very interesting, and when you visit it, as you should, do not forget to leave a donation, for museums like this depend on one.

Throughout all this part of the Highlands there are many National Trust for Scotland properties and National Nature Reserves. One cannot praise these places too highly: they do a most excellent job in preserving for our children some of the fragile beauties and wonders of the country. And they are fragile: even the highest and stoniest mountain can be changed and ruined by those who love it and visit it often.

And yet these oases of preservation are embedded in an area where everything is beauty, except for what has happened to the people. Of course lip service is paid to the necessity of keeping people alive in the Highlands and preserving the communities, but there is little practical effort, and the drift to the cities and the south continues, for there is as yet no alternative.

And still the agricultural land, the once fertile glens and straths, year by year go back to rushes and heather, and the croft houses bear a harvest of Bed and Breakfast signs, and the best crop a crofter can gather is a couple of caravans on the in-bye grazing.

It is time, and more than time, that as much attention be paid to the conservancy of people as to the conservancy of nature.

CHAPTER 2

Oykel Bridge, Achiltibuie, Inverkirkaig, Lochinver, Kylestrome

THE ROAD NORTH FROM Ullapool (A835) is wide and fast. Beside it here and there you can see the old road, and those who remember that old road are perhaps somewhat nostalgic about it, for narrow and twisting though it was, travelling it you did have time to savour the fantastic mountains – Suilven, Canisp, Stac Polly, Cul Mor – which rear up from the moorland, itself bedecked with lochans.

It cannot be their height which makes these mountains so

Stac Polly from Loch Lurgainn

very special, for the highest, Ben More Assynt, is only 3,273 feet. They are all individuals, not a range of mountains, and seem to act like individuals, each standing in solitude, almost glaring across the wide moors at its neighbours.

These are the survivors, the last remnants, of some unimaginably great mountain range of many millions of years ago. Everything else has been swept away, leaving these gnarled old warriors behind. They even seem to move as the road winds between them – Stac Polly peers between Coigach and Cul Beag; Suilven overlooks Cul Mor; Canisp slips behind Suilven. All very strange and weird.

About twelve miles north of Ullapool is the Inverpolly National Nature Reserve, with an information centre at Knockan Cliff, just by the road. This Reserve covers almost 27,000 acres of some of the wildest and least inhabited country in Scotland.

Much of it is privately owned, but the estates co-operate in maintaining the untamed and untouched land. There are high mountains – Cul Mor and Cul Beag and Stac Polly. There is Loch Sionascaig. And the Reserve runs all the way to the distant west coast in a glorious expanse of scree and loch, moorland and mountain and deserted sea shore. Within the wide range of habitats there is a great variety of wildlife and a great variety of flora, and the purpose of the Reserve is to permit this variety to evolve with the minimum of interference by man. There is a Nature Trail to be followed, and a very interesting Geology Trail following the Moine Thrust, where the imperceptible movement of great rock plates can be studied. Mountains, moorland, woodland, water – an unforgettable offering of unspoiled beauty to be visited and enjoyed.

However, if you follow that fine wild road (A837) direct to the north, you will miss roads to the west that take you through even wilder and lovelier country.

There is a minor road to the left, about eight miles north of Ullapool, and if you follow that it takes you the length of Loch Lurgainn, beneath Cul Beag and Stac Polly and finally back to the coast at dramatic Achnahaird Bay. Go straight on at the road junction, again across a wild and desolate moor down to the coast, and you come to a sea dotted with the entrancing Summer Isles, a treasure poured out carelessly like some casket of jewels. It is an enchanted scene, a scene of beauty very precious indeed.

The road winds down the coast, and over bare moors to the tiny settlement of Achiltibuie, and then continues again, finally ending at Culnacraig. At Achiltibuie you will find a smokery which produces smoked salmon and other products. You are welcome to visit (and to buy, of course), and you surely will not be disappointed if you do. Try the freshly smoked salmon cut thick, not as a transparent sliver, and experience a new sensation of flavour.

There are boat trips from Achiltibuie to Tanera Mor, one of the Summer Isles, and it is possible to arrange visits to others. Tanera Mor once supported seventy people, but the last of them left in 1946, and now there are no permanent inhabitants.

There was a large fishing station there in the 18th century, and contemporary prints show it as a thriving community with quite large vessels anchored off-shore.

These isles are a paradise for naturalists. Seals and a host of sea birds breed there. Twenty-nine varieties have been reported on Priest Island alone. Today the islands are used as sheep grazings, the sheep being ferried out in the spring and back to the mainland for winter. Tanera Mor was once the home of Fraser Darling, the great naturalist whose studies of deer and bird life added so much to our knowledge.

There is a track from the road end at Culnacraig, and it follows the delightful coast closely, round Camas Mor, to join the main road again at Strathcanaird, on the A835 north of Ullapool.

The road north from Achiltibuie does not go far, and ends at Reiff, which has a fine sandy beach backed by cliffs, and is a very pleasant place to spend a happy day. Actually, you can reach Isle Ristol, one of the Summer Isles, on foot from just south of Allt an Dubh. There is a causeway to the island, but you must be careful, because you can use it only at low tide.

**The Achiltibuie
Hydroponicum Ltd.**

*Achilitibuie, Ross-shire
IV26 2YG
Tel: 01854 622202
Fax: 01854 622201*
E-mail:
hydroponicum.info@virgin.net
Internet web site:
http://www.race.co.uk./hydroponicum

THE HYDROPONICUM is the UK's first soil-less indoor garden! Step into a different world of lush, sub-tropical fruit trees, flowers and vegetables.

Enjoy the relaxing atmosphere of the Lilypond Cafe, whilst indulging in fresh hydroponic produce, home cooking and baking. The Hydroponic Gift Shop offers a variety of hydro-ponic growing kits & accessories. Mail order is available throughout the year.

Picnic Lawns   Parking   Hourly guided tours

Open Daily 10am – 6pm   Easter – 30 September

There are many very fine walks around this coast, and if you are staying here, the hotelier is a mine of information. He will also tell you about the remarkable 'Hydroponicum' which you cannot help seeing from the hotel, and wondering about. It is a strange construction, incongruous in its Highland setting, but fascinating. Here plants are grown without soil, with their roots bathed in a solution of nutrients and warmed by solar panels. All very strange, but visit it (there are tours) and perhaps you will have seen the future working.

You must return more or less the way you came, but there is a loop road, clearly marked on the maps, which takes you over moorland and past lochs back to the road junction by Achnahaird Bay. Past Loch Osgaig, and just at the edge of Loch Bad a Ghaill a road to the left heads due north for Inverkirkaig and Loch Inver.

There is a grand viewpoint at this road junction, looking

over the wastelands of Inverpolly Forest, and with Stac Polly looming over myriad lochs and lochans sprinkled on the bare moors. This road north is narrow and twisting and slow, but it is quite superb, travelling over moors of every tweed colour, swooping down to touch the rock-bound coast at Enard Bay then climbing again over high moors and dropping down to Inverkirkaig. It is a grand road indeed, and one that seems to capture the very essence of the Highlands in all its romance, beauty and tragedy. There is not much to Inverkirkaig itself except a fine waterfall nearby, but there is a very good bookshop, and it is as astonishing to find that there as it would be to discover a real diamond ring in a Christmas cracker. But the Highlands never cease to astonish.

You find the waterfall by following the track up the river Kirkaig to Fionn Loch. It is a most enjoyable jaunt, and, if you wish, you can go beyond the falls, following a much fainter track, to the summit of Suilven, that strange mass of stone, 2,399 feet high, which is so well known as 'The Sugar Loaf'.

Suilven always looks threatening and impregnable to the walker, but in fact it is a bit of a softy, and presents no real problem to any walker who is properly equipped.

North from Inverkirkaig to Lochinver the road continues its spectacular progress, with fine views of the great Torridon mountains – Suilven, Canisp, Cul Mor and Coigach amongst them – rearing like great beasts from the moors.

Lochinver is a popular holiday resort, and can be busy; it is also a working fishing port. One of the great attractions of Lochinver is that a wealth of delightful sandy coves are close by, most of them a few miles north on the Stoer Peninsula, a place reminiscent of the Isles, rather than the mainland. The roads to the crofting villages where those coves lie are narrow, and twist grandly across moors strewn with lochans. There are stretches of machair here and there, the lovely grass sward growing so precariously on sand dunes, and in spring jewelled with a remarkable display of wild flowers. The machair, though, is very delicate, and cannot withstand the constant trampling of human feet, even less the battering from cars and caravans, and it has suffered sadly, even fatally, over the years. Just the same, most of the crofting villages are attractive, and they have delightful names – Achmelvich, Clashnessie, Clachtoll, Stoer, Culkein.

The road on the west side of the Stoer peninsula ends by the lighthouse at Raffin, but a track goes on from there for two miles or so to Stoer Point and its dramatic rock pillar, the Old Man of Stoer. This great rock pillar, all 200 feet of it, stands just off-shore, perpetually foam-ringed and seeming inaccessible.

Incredible though it seems, the rock has been climbed, first in 1961 and occasionally since. It is a most impressive sight, with the great cliffs, 300 feet high, ringing it, and this pillar of rock challenging alone the full force of every gale.

The peninsula takes its name from the rock pillar, which comes from the Norse Staurr, or The Stake, and the Gaels added Rbha or headland. This combina-

Golden Eagle

tion of Norse and Gaelic is not uncommon, and the further north you go, the more common it becomes.

You will find many fulmars nesting hereabouts, and if you climb the prominent hill by the lighthouse, you will be rewarded with another of those quite stupendous views of sea, islands, lochs and mountains, mountains stretching far to the east, even to Ben Wyvis.

The views of mountains from Lochinver itself are also very fine, and one could never tire of the lovely dark shapes looming against a bright sky. With its combination of excellent beaches and delightful walking, Lochinver's popularity can well be understood.

For walkers, if they should weary of the endless beauties of the coast, there are just as fine walks inland, especially through Glen Canisp and Glencanisp Forest, right up to (and to the top of, if you wish) the sugar loaf of Suilven.

There is a choice of roads north from Lochinver. One can keep to the coast road by Drumbeg (B869) or go east by A837 to Loch Assynt before turning north again to Kylestrome on A894. I would not miss either, even if a certain amount of back-tracking must be done.

The tiny coast road is a miracle of delight, with new views and prospects every mile, and every prospect a pleasure. To the left is the enchanting Eddrachillis Bay and its wealth of islands. To the right and ahead is a great outpouring of mountains and moors and lochs. It is quite wonderful, if you are not the driver on this difficult road, and a pleasure rare indeed.

Equally, the road from Lochinver to Loch Assynt and the north is an exhilarating experience, crossing the great moors, passing a wealth of lochs, and then running down the length of Loch Assynt to Skiag Bridge.

Here and there on the moors and on the flanks of the hills are bright green patches, contrasting vividly in summer with the subdued colours which predominate. The patches mark the sites of the old shielings, the summer grazings of the old days, where the livestock and the women spent the summer, while the men worked a crop off the lower arable land. The green is not grass today, as it once was, but bracken, and the land now feeds nothing.

Assynt is a name well marked in Highland history, and saw many a struggle between rival clans. It was a sad time, but through it all, as the remains of the shielings show, the life and comparative prosperity of the people persisted. It was when outside influences forced themselves into these hills that the fragile society shattered.

All this area was once the great Reay Forest, owned (although that is not absolutely correct, for these were all clan lands) by Lord Reay. He sold in 1829 to George Leveson-Gower for £300,000. Immediately Leveson-Gower became the most hated man in Scotland, for he cleared off about 15,000 people to make way for sheep. Hated or not, he was rewarded by his King, for William IV made him the Duke of Sutherland in 1833, and he and his Duchess continued their rape of the Highlands throughout Sutherland.

Capercaillie

Halfway along Loch Assynt, close to where the road (A837) comes up from Inchnadamph, there are the few poor remains of Ardvreck Castle. A notable part of Scottish history saw an ignoble end here, for it was at Ardvreck that the Great Montrose was confined before being taken to Edinburgh for execution.

Montrose is one of the great luminous figures who from time to time have flashed across the Scottish skies. It is not ridiculous to place him alongside Wallace and Bruce. Montrose, like them, was a military genius, and he brought his genius to bear in efforts to keep the Stuarts on the throne. It was the time of the Covenanting Wars and the Civil War, a time of confusion and mixed loyalties. But Montrose was not confused, and he struck hard time and again at the enemies of the Stuarts, especially the Campbells in distant Inveraray.

His last campaign was a tragedy, though, for, in exile, he sought to place Charles II on the throne. He landed first in Orkney, then moved to Caithness and south, but at Carbisdale his small force was taken by surprise and scattered. Montrose sought shelter at Ardvreck but was betrayed and captured there.

He met his death with rare dignity and courage, but the cause for which he died survived, and led to the Jacobite risings of the 18th century.

Neil McLeod of Assynt, who betrayed Montrose, was rewarded by a grateful government with £20,000 Scots (not much) and 400 bolls of meal, which was sour.

The McLeods of Assynt have held land around the Loch from the time of Bannockburn, when the last of the McNicol line married a McLeod of Lewis, a long history indeed to have reached such a nadir with the egregious Neil.

In the records of the Seaforths, there is an account of a clan raid, 'a great depredation at Assynt'. The Seaforths carried off 2,400 cows, 1,500 horses, about 6,000 sheep and goats 'besides that he burned and destroyed many families.' When one looks today at those empty glens and hillsides, lovely though they certainly are, it is difficult to escape a sense of haunting sadness for the past, when those same hills were rich with cattle and children.

Inchnadamph is at the eastern end of Loch Assynt, and although there is little of it to be seen today, one of the most important archaeological discoveries in Scotland was made there in 1926.

There is a group of four caves in the limestone, and when they were excavated many bones of arctic animals were found: reindeer, cave bear, lynx and arctic fox. There were burned stones and bones, charcoal and incised bones and antlers, as well as two carefully buried skeletons. These were the remains of the earliest known inhabitants of Scotland, from 11,000 years ago.

Actually, there are traces of ancient man all over the moors of Assynt. They are difficult for the layman to see, and certainly cannot be seen from a car. They are the remains of chamber burial cairns, mostly, of a people and society of whom we know nothing.

The road (A837) south-east from Loch Assynt to Lairg and Bonar Bridge is very fine. It is a lonely road, again over high moors with many lochans. There is one especially fine viewpoint a few miles past Altnacealgach where the road has taken one of its great sweeps up the side of a hill. You can recognise it because it is just before you reach some of the scarce woodlands on the road. There is a great panorama of mountains, all the mountains you have been seeing for so many miles, but now from a different viewpoint. Cul Mor, Suilven, Canisp, even, in the distance, Ben More Assynt – a circlet of mountains breathtaking in their beauty.

Further north the A894 runs up to Kylesku and Unapool. The ferry there used to be a dreaded bottleneck on the road north or south, but it has gone now, and has been replaced by a bridge. Even though waiting for the ferry used to be the source of much frustration, at least it did allow you to look around and enjoy the fine situation, a pleasure denied if you simply roar over the bridge and away.

Waiting for the ferry was also a good opportunity to watch the seals which seemed to congregate round the slipway. They still do, although the ferry has gone. You can sit at breakfast in the hotel and watch them playing.

Three lochs meet here, Loch Cairnbawn, Loch Glendhu and Loch Glencoul, and the views of Quinag, Glas Bheinn and Beinn Leoid are grand.

The highest waterfall in Britain is at the head of Loch Glencoul, but it needs an effort to get there, unless you take one of the boat trips from Kylesku. Personally, I feel that is too easy, and that the way to enjoy places such as Eas Coul Aulin is to walk there.

It is not too difficult, by Loch Glencoul, although there is no track really, and you will be walking steep grassy slopes above some sheer drops – not perhaps for the vertiginous. There is a track from the main road near Loch na Gaimnlich, south of the village. There is also a much longer track from Inchnadamph, but that does not have a great deal to recommend it.

The falls are most impressive after rain, when their roar is deafening. They drop 658 feet, although not in one leap, and you will see how they get their lovely name of The Maiden's Tresses from the way in which the falling water is dashed into a million gleaming parts as it meets the hard rocks.

Another excellent walk from near Kylesku takes you due east up Loch Glendhu, and, if you wish, over the moors as far as Kinloch on the A838 road between Laxford Bridge and Lairg. It is from this track that you might best appreciate the name of 'Quinag', whose bulk looms away to the south-west, because from that track it does slightly resemble the water stoup from which its name derives.

CHAPTER 3

Kylesku, Scourie, Handa Island, Loch Laxford, Kinlochbervie, Cape Wrath and Durness

NORTH FROM KYLESKU THE road (still A894) goes on to Scourie across the enchanting Eddrachillis Bay, with wild mountain and moorland on the other side of the road. This is indeed a road of rare delight; it is not a road to be driven at speed, but to be taken slowly and savoured, like a fine malt whisky.

Sunset over Eddrachillis Bay is worth waiting for, as the sun disappears over the far Hebrides, leaving all the islands silhouetted black against a sky radiant with a thousand colours, and the hills to the east brilliant in their greens and browns.

Badcall Bay

The village of Scourie is the local metropolis, a typical and charming crofting village, with an excellent sandy beach. Deservedly, it is a popular holiday centre for walkers, anglers and bird watchers especially, and has much to offer them all. The walker has seemingly endless miles of coast and moor to walk; the angler a vast variety of hill lochs; the bird watcher has the coast, and, close by, Handa Island.

Sailors, too, find Eddrachillis Bay a great attraction, with a wealth of fine uninhabited islands to visit, one for each day of the year, so it is claimed.

These seas can be treacherous, though, open as they are to the peculiar fury of the Minch. During the war, other sailors on other business used the bay, for it was here the British midget submarines gathered, and the crews trained. Those who survived and survive to this day have many tales of mild adventure and mishap round the islands. But it was from here that the small flotilla of tiny submarines, each towed by a mother submarine of full size, left for the successful attack on the Tirpitz in a Norwegian fiord. Few returned.

At Scourie (Gaelic: *Sgobhairigh* – Shieling by the Little Wood) the A894 swings away to the north-east, on its last lap to the north, the end of the road, the very north of Scotland. But there are some side trips first.

Just north of Scourie a minor road off to the left heads for Tarbet, Handa Island and Loch Laxford. Don't ignore it. It is a narrow, thrilling road crossing wild moors and going by tiny lochs; it is a colourful road of unfailing delight.

Tarbet, at the end of the road, is a lovely little crofting village, typical of the villages carved out of inhospitable nature by those deprived of their better, kinder land 150 years ago. A passenger ferry from Tarbet goes over to Handa Island.

The island is a bird sanctuary, and is under the care of the Royal Society for the Protection of Birds. There is a bothy on the island, and members of RSPB can stay there by arrangement, but no one else is permitted to camp there, and rightly so.

About a dozen families once lived on the island, and like the families of St Kilda and other rocky islands, made much of their diet from sea birds and their eggs, and developed a fine, reckless skill in scrambling over the terrifying cliffs to collect their food.

Handa Island

There was a 'Queen' of Handa, too, and a 'Parliament' which met daily and decided the tasks for the day. This was necessary, for almost none of the work, especially cliff climbing, could be done by one man alone, but demanded a team. The potato blight ended human occupation of Handa, and the people, those few left, emigrated to America.

Handa Island is about 760 acres of Torridonian sandstone, edged with dramatic cliffs, some 400 feet high. The interior of the island, mostly a high plateau, is peaty and has several lochans. There is good sheep pasture, and some machair, which, in the absence of all vehicles and most people, grows in rich and verdant beauty. But it is for the birds that you would visit Handa, for here they breed and live in safety and peace. Guillemots, kittiwakes, razorbills, puffins, fulmar, shags – no less than 150 species have been recorded on Handa, and no less than forty-five breed there. As an example, 25-30,000 pairs of guillemots.

It is the skuas you need to watch out for on Handa, for they never cease their dive-bombing attacks. The best time to visit the island is June and early July, because after that the birds begin to migrate.

If the weather permits, local boatmen often offer trips right round Handa, and that is an easy way to appreciate its soaring cliffs. You will also see the Stack, another of those remarkable off-shore pillars of rock. There are only a few yards of swirling water between the Stack and the foot of the cliffs, but you would have to go down about 500 feet to cross those few yards.

Loch Laxford is just around the corner of Rubha Ruadh – Red Point – from Tarbet and Handa, and certainly should be visited. It is a deep fiord running far into the mainland, almost as far as Rhiconich, and it is quite lovely. Island-studded and romantic, it is also quiet: balm indeed for the troubled mind.

However, there is of course a fly in the healing ointment of Loch Laxford, for here, as in so many Highland lochs today, fish farming has intruded.

There can be no argument about the value of fish farming: it is (although possibly temporarily) offering economic help to an area that desperately needs it. But one must ask why it has to be so untidy and uncaring, not everywhere, it is true, but in too many places. New endeavours of this kind should complement, not compete with, older economic activities, and not the least important of those is tourism, on which the Highlands has perforce come to rely. Tourists are not entranced by a mass of industrial rubbish.

It is also reasonable to give a thought to how the salmon in those off-shore cages are reared. Many thousands of fish spend their short lives confined there, in conditions at least as crowded and inhumane as experienced by any unfortunate battery chicken. Apart from the pollution which is so visible on shore, the sea bed is also being polluted and sterilised. You will perhaps have noticed that salmon is now on sale, quite cheaply, in every supermarket. The fish came from these cages, and have lived out their lives – those that survive long enough to reach the killing box – in crowded conditions of considerable stress and total artificiality.

From Tarbet and Loch Laxford you must return to the main

Ben Stack by Scourie

road (A894) again for the north, past Baluabay and over Laxford Bridge, where again there are superb views down Loch Laxford.

Laxford Bridge is just that, a bridge over the river Laxford. As you might guess from its name, the Laxford is a fabled salmon river (*Lax* is Norse for salmon) and must have been for centuries.

There is a road junction here, and the A838 comes in from the south-east, from distant Lairg. Now that is a fine and quiet road, almost forty miles of it running past loch after loch, mountain after mountain and hardly a house on it. By Loch Stack, Loch More, Loch Merkland, Loch a'Ghriama and finally Loch Shin, the road takes you the length of them all, through what is virtually one long valley.

The road, grand though it is, does not measure up, perhaps, to the grandeur of the coast road, but then that is comparing the excellent and the sublime.

Few tracks can attract the walker off that road to Lairg, but there is one, a long-distance path through the hills to faraway Strath More, where it joins up with another minor road between Altnaharra and the north. That track begins just at the north end of Loch Merkland, and wanders through deep glens, between high hills and by very remote lochs. It is a fine track and one which sees few walkers. At its northern end it passes by the foot of the strangely named (to English ears) Glen Golly.

The road we are following, though, turns north here, and there are a few miles to travel that are remarkable even in this country. To right and left of the road is empty country, cut and faceted with countless lochs and hills. It is difficult to know what is inland and what is sea, what is sea and which is sky. It is indeed a lovely place, at least when the sun shines. On a day of driving rain, which is not unknown, it it is as dour a place as you will find. But the sun always shines again, and when it does, the hills and lochs are like a great enamel fresh from the furnace, bright and gleaming.

At Rhiconich a minor but good road (B801) leads off to the left, to Kinlochbervie and beyond. It runs very finely along the length of Loch Inchard, and at one point, about 2 miles from the beginning of the loch, where the road has soared high above the water, is a splendid viewpoint across the loch to the wilderness of loch-strewn moorland to the south.

Kinlochbervie is a busy fishing port, and still expanding. Actually, there are two harbours. The old one is a bit decrepit now, and a spanking new one, sheltered by a high hill, is still being expanded. There are fish processing plants here, too, and associated activities, and altogether Kinlochbervie is a fine and thriving little place. Although most of the boats are effectively based at Kinlochbervie, many of the fishermen are not. Mostly they are east coast men, and there is the long-established practice that when the boats have unloaded their last catch on a Friday, the crews take off by bus or car to their homes in the east, returning very early on Monday morning.

The road continues beyond the village, three miles or so to Sheigra, past some delightful sands at Oldshore Mor. This is crofting country, but that must be a hard life here especially, trying to wring crops from the peaty soil during the short summers.

Beyond the road end, a track continues to Sandwood Bay. It is not an easy track to walk and walk you must, crossing peat bogs and empty moorland, past the stack rock of An Buachaille, the Herdsman. The reward, though, is great, for Sandwood Bay is a fine arc of glorious sand, almost certainly empty and untrodden.

This is the place where most of the shipwrecks of Cape Wrath ended up, from the time before the lighthouse was built, carried by currents, and the remains are still there. A mermaid used to live on off-shore rocks, and she was seen many times by shepherds, but not recently.

Perhaps, in spite of the great beauty of Sandwood Bay, you

will feel a certain uneasiness, maybe of spirit, while you are there. You will not be the first to feel this, and indeed it has been commented on for centuries. It is an indefinable feeling of dread, as though a slight haze has crossed the sun on a fine summer's day, but strong enough with many people to cause them to leave the bay to its mermaid, its loneliness and its memories of shipwreck.

You must go back the same way, through Kinlochbervie, and on to Rhiconich, for the final stretch leading to the far north, Durness and Cape Wrath itself. The road runs north-east from Rhiconich, where you finally leave the sea of the Hebrides. The next salt water will be Kyle of Durness.

The road takes you over moorland, climbing and falling, with good views of the vast empty Parph, with Cape Wrath at the tip. Parph is another Norse word meaning 'Turning', for it was at that point that the Norse ships turned to the south for the richness the west coast offered them.

This whole area, of course, is Sutherland, which means no more than Southland, but it is a strange name for the most northerly area of Scotland. It was a Norse name, of course, and to the Norse, this was indeed their 'Southland'. The north-east they called Caithness – the promontory of Cat. They controlled the whole area then, in the post-Roman times, and began actually settling, as distinct from raiding, in the 8th century.

Originally Pictish country, the Picts were not, of course, exterminated. Many of them would have survived the invasion, pressing down beneath the nearest rock while the waves of war washed over them, as people have always done, and do to this day. Women were things of value, and would generally be preserved, and ultimately the blood of conqueror and conquered would mingle, as it has always done. Even the old Celtic Christianity did not vanish, for the Norse took over many of the holy places and stones, and used them for their own worship of Thor and Odin.

Cape Wrath

You cannot reach Cape Wrath by car, or at least not your own car. There is a passenger ferry from just south of Durness, and then you must take a waiting mini-bus for the eleven-mile trip across exceptionally barren moors to the Cape itself.

There is a lighthouse at Cape Wrath designed, like so many others in Scotland, by the father of Robert Louis Stevenson. It stands high on cliffs of remarkable splendour and beauty. But we can imagine that in a winter gale the Cape earns its name of Cape Wrath. See it in its summer beauty, though, and take delight in it. The cliffs are multi-coloured, with veins of pink running through the dark Lewisian gneiss. And the wild flowers gladden the heart: sea pinks, primula scotia and a host of others.

There are sea birds too, in vast numbers, and you will probably see gannets diving into the constantly churning waters. They may well have come all the way from their nesting place on distant St Kilda to take their meal here.

A mile or so to the north of the lighthouse are the great cliffs of Clo-mor, amongst the highest in Britain, and the breeding ground of razorbills, kittiwakes, puffins and guillemots.

From the little hill just by the lighthouse there is a glorious view up and down the rugged coast, and in the distance lovely and remote Sandwood Bay. On a clear day you can just see the Hebrides on the far horizon and, if you are very lucky, the distant Orkneys. However, if you face due north, there is nothing but a vast stretch of water between you and the North Pole.

All in all, the trip to Cape Wrath is very much worth while, not only for the immense satisfaction of standing on the north-western tip of Scotland, but for the sheer beauty, the untamed wildness, of it all. Apart from the lighthouse, itself as solid as a cliff, there are no concessions here to man: this is nature, the sea and the wind and the rain, and man is as nothing compared to such tremendous and eternal forces.

Durness is a small village, but is naturally a considerable tourist attraction, since it is the most north-westerly village in Scotland, and the turning point for visitors. From the south, the approach is over bleak moorland, but then quite abruptly there is a change to good green grass, a land clearly much richer. That abrupt change shows the boundaries of the great outcrop of Durness limestone, which provides a much kindlier soil than the sour peat of the moorland.

This land has been farmed and cherished for centuries, from the time of the Picts onwards; there are the scant remains of two Pictish towers, possibly brochs, just south of Durness. The Picts invariably chose good agricultural land for their settlements, and built their brochs to protect it. This land has been farmed constantly since those distant days.

This richer land was, naturally, envied by those who sought to clear the people and make way for sheep, but in fact there were no clearances here, and the local legend about that is interesting. It seems that the sheriff officer did in fact come to Durness with orders for clearances, and, as usual, he timed his arrival carefully so that only the women and children were there, for the men were about their business on the hill. The sheriff, though, had miscalculated, for the women of Durness knew well what had happened elsewhere, and were prepared to fight for their land. They did not wish to use force, though, to dispossess the sheriff of his order, so they merely held his hand, clutching his official papers, over a fire until he himself dropped them in the flames. Thus they won a reprieve, which turned out to be permanent.

It is a story which could well be true, for the crofting women have always been strong in defence of their homes and land. It was usually the women who faced police and troops, and drove them back in the Crofting War of the mid-19th century.

Apart from the unending beauty of its surroundings, perhaps the most exciting thing at Durness is the remarkable Balnakeil Craft Village. It is a rather unprepossessing assembly of obviously military huts, now turned into a haven for craftspeople of all kinds.

It was a camp designed as an Early Warning System (one of those peculiar installations designed to give us three, rather than two minutes to prepare to meet our end) but had become obsolete by the time it was completed, and so was abandoned by the military before they had properly occupied it. After some time, and with great imagination, it was acquired by the County Council, who sought to use it first as a centre for industry.

Only craft workers were really interested, though, and they

moved in, taking over the huts and producing their craftwork of many kinds. Thirty years later, craftspeople are still there, in perhaps the greatest concentration of craft skills anywhere in Britain.

The village has been prettified; there is an exhibition and a tea room, and an excellent hotel, and it is all highly impressive, even though, in spite of every effort, a military camp can never be beautiful. There is a quite astonishing variety of skills displayed there, producing goods for sale, and you have the chance to see the goods actually being produced and to talk to the craftspeople making them. Do not miss it.

It is sad, though, to notice how few of those skilled, energetic and enterprising people are Scots.

Balnakeil actually means 'Place of the Church', and the first Christian establishment there was as early as the 8th century. Like so many others, it was set up by Mael Rubha.

The ruins of the church we see today at Balnakeil, though, go back only to 1619, when it was built on the ruins of an earlier church, which was in turn built on one even earlier, and that may have been the cell of Mael Rubha.

There is a monument in the churchyard to the memory of Rob Donn Calder, or Mackay (1714-1778), a great Gaelic poet, although he was illiterate, like so many others. Those who know the work of both have compared Rob Donn to Robert Burns. Like the mother of Burns, Rob Donn's mother had a wealth of songs and stories to which he listened intently as a child, and which provided him with material as a poet. He was a cowherd and drover, and is said to have been a notable poacher. He was a guest at all local weddings and celebrations, not so much because he was particularly popular, but rather because if he was not invited, some scurrilous verse of his about the occasion would be doing the rounds within the week.

Rob Donn never saw his poems in print, but they were printed two years after his death, and the next year there was the publication of a translation into English, with an introduction by Sir Walter Scott, no less.

Another stone in the churchyard has a very odd commentary on the life and death of Donald Macmurchow:

DONALD MACMURCHOW HIER LYIS LO
VAS IL TO HIS FREIND, VAR TO HIS FO.
TRVE TO HIS MAISTER IN VEIRD AND VO...1623
(*var,* worse; *veird,* prosperity.)

There is most excellent walking from Durness, and one of the best walks is through the dunes from Balnakeil to what some maps show as 'Far Out Head'. This in fact is *Fear Ard*, or

Smoo Caves

High Fellow, and is a headland, 300 feet high above the sea, with glorious views of cliffs and island-bedecked sea, round to Loch Eriboll and Whiten Head, over to Cape Wrath and south to the hills of the Reay Forest. The dunes and cliffs are the home of myriad seabirds, including many puffins.

Golfers should note that Durness is the home of mainland Scotland's most northerly course, and a fine one it is. There is one remarkable hole, a 155 yard shot over the Atlantic! Yes, it's true, as you can see for yourself. Another interesting thing about the Durness course is the rule that players must not disturb anglers fishing on Loch Lanlish.

You would be wise to follow that rule, because I can well see that any interruption to fishing that delectable loch could lead to recriminations or worse.

The Smoo Caves are one of the great attractions of Durness. They are great caverns in the limestone cliffs just east of the village, where the Smoo burn dives underground. The caves are easily approached by a short track down to the beach from the roadside, and the first cavern is immensely impressive, with a great entrance arch 50 feet high. The cavern is over 200 feet long and 130 feet wide.

The second and third caverns are not so easy of approach. Indeed, many books say that the third is impossible to enter. That is not quite so, but it certainly needs preparation, especially lights. The second cavern can be entered easily enough, so long as you are prepared to get wet, for its entrance is over a rock wall over which the Smoo burn tumbles into a deepish pool. It is a case, really, of trainers and no trousers. When you get inside, there is a fine cave, seventy feet by thirty feet, with two openings in the roof, and the burn pours down one of them.

The third compartment, which is beyond the second, is a squeeze to enter, and is totally dark, about 120 feet long and eight feet wide and varies up to perhaps forty feet high. There are many stalactites, although not particularly attractive ones, being dark brown, and not the gleaming white of other caves.

One of the best descriptions of the Smoo Caves was written by Sir Walter Scott in his diary for 19th September 1814. The fact that the not particularly energetic Sir Walter was able to explore all three caves shows that they are indeed approachable.

CHAPTER 4

Loch Eribol, Loch Hope, Loch Loyal, Tongue, Bettyhill, Altnaharra, Lairg, Croick

FROM DURNESS OUR ROUTE goes in a zigzag fashion to Bettyhill, before turning definitively south to Lairg and Inverness. It would be wasted opportunity to take the most direct route to Bettyhill, unless time is very pressing indeed. Instead, after going round Loch Eribol, head south on the unclassified road running down Loch Hope, past Dun Dornaigil broch almost to Altnaharra. Swing north again there for Tongue, and then east to Bettyhill before going south on B871 and B873 for Altnaharra and then A836 for Lairg and the south. I can promise you that you will not regret taking this route.

Local initiative has produced a very informative and useful leaflet for visitors to this area, and it is very much worth while picking it up from the Information Centre. It not only gives the interesting derivation of the strange, half-Norse names of villages and geographical features, but also outlines a number of walks and trips, and guides the casual visitor to fascinating places that are easy to miss.

Loch Eribol was well known to many thousands of servicemen during the last war as Lock 'Orrible, and with some reason. There was nothing there then but military and naval establishments and a desecrated beauty. Today, that which was foreign has gone, leaving only what was always there – a beauty rare and delightful. On a day of bright sunshine, at any time of the year, Loch Eribol and its cradling mountains is a most wonderful pastiche of colour and texture. Add to that the smell of heather and seaweed and the sound of waves and seabirds and you have a total delight for the senses, a delight so rare and precious that it can almost be painful. Loch Eribol is beautiful, and there is nothing more to say.

There is no road, nor even a real track from the eastern shore of Loch Eribol to Whiten Head, where the loch meets the Pentland Firth, but it is possible to walk there, along the cliffs, and it is a fine and most exhilarating walk and not a stroll. There are caves under the cliffs at Whiten Head, and the Atlantic Grey Seal breeds there, the only known breeding place on the mainland.

Just where the road swings round the head of the Loch, under the great and listen to the astonishing slopes of Creag na Faolinn, shout loudly, and listen to the astonishing series of echoes.

The road down Loch Hope passes through some rich farmland, and beef cattle flourish in good grass there. It is a startling contrast to see cattle and richness after so many miles of sheep and land on which man must struggle to raise a crop of any sort.

To the east of the road is the high peak of Ben Hope, the most northerly 'Munro' (mountain over 3,000 feet) in Scotland, and there is a fine waterfall, Allt-na-caillich, just beyond the loch.

Dun Dornaigil Broch is there, another of those lovely Pictish towers raised so long ago, and so ingeniously, as a defensive position against raiders. Dun Dornaigil has been carefully preserved (not restored), and you cannot enter it, but it is still most impressive, not least for the great triangular lintel above the doorway. When you look at the good farmland all around the broch, you realise again just how our Pictish ancestors so care-

Dun Dornaigil Broch

fully chose the places where they lived. There is good grazing land, there is a fine river, there are defensive mountains. No doubt about it, they knew what they were doing, all those 2000 years ago.

Our route turns northward at the junction with the Altnaharra Tongue road (A836), after passing through some rather dreary forestry plantings, and then, more interestingly, running along the shore of Loch Loyal, under the ridge of shapely Ben Loyal to Tongue.

There is, of course, a much shorter route to Tongue from Loch Eribol, straight across the moors, then, surprisingly, over a causeway and bridge crossing the Kyle of Tongue itself. It is a good road, and pleasant, but it is in no way to be compared with the long circuit down Loch Hope and up Loch Loyal.

Tongue is a green and well-wooded village, a strange contrast in many ways to the austerity of most of these northern communities.

This is Reay country, of the Clan Mackay, and Tongue House, just north of the village, was once the home of the Lords of Reay. It was Sir Donald Mackay of Farr who became the first Lord Reay in 1628, and he was a wizard and well known for it. He had repeated dealings with the Devil himself, and the Devil did not always come off best.

One day, exercising his wizardry in distant Padua (why, I know not), Sir Donald went too far in his dealings with the Devil, and was chased all the way back to Sutherland before he could find the necessary wizardry to throw his pursuer off the scent.

Varich Castle stands on a hill above Tongue, but there is little left of it today – just a few walls – and indeed little is known of it. The name indicates a Norse origin, and it is reputed to have been the stronghold of some Norse warrior of the 11th century. A track from the village leads up to the ruins, and the views over the Kyle alone would make it a worthwhile stroll.

Just south of Tongue, on the narrow road round the Kyle, a road little travelled now since the opening of the causeway, there is a monument to Ewan Robertson, who is known as 'The Bard of the Clearances'. He died at a nearby croft in 1895. He wrote:

In place of the sheep there will be people,
Cattle with shielings in place of stags.

Well, the Bard's hopeful vision has not been fulfilled, almost a hundred years after his death, but that is not to say it will never happen.

The road from Tongue (still A836) doglegs north, then east,

then north again to Bettyhill and Farr, but unless you are once again in a great hurry, a very pleasant detour goes off the main road to the left, out again to the north coast, then circles back round to regain the main road at Borgie Bridge. It is the usual narrow highland road, but quite charming, running past tiny lochs, through hardwoods (and what a pleasant change they make to the ranks of conifers), and past very fine beaches.

In March 1746, the Kyle of Tongue was the scene of a naval battle that probably sealed the fate of Prince Charles Edward and the Jacobite Rebellion. With the withdrawal of the Jacobite forces north to Inverness, they were desperately short of food and money. Urgent appeals to the French King eventually produced a rather grudging response, and he sent off £13,600 in gold pieces, and a small detachment of Jacobite soldiers. They were despatched in a sloop, once the *H.M.S. Hazard*, which had been captured, and renamed, naturally, the *Prince Charles*.

By ill chance, the *Prince Charles* was sighted by the English navy, and chased by a squadron up the east coast and right through the Pentland Firth. Closely pursued by the frigate *Sheerness*, the *Prince Charles* sailed right into the Kyle of Tongue, hoping that the larger English ship would be unable to follow. The *Prince Charles*, though, went aground just by Ard Skinnid, within gunshot of the *Sheerness*. They exchanged fire, and the smaller ship was disabled.

When darkness fell, the Jacobites landed with the treasure, intending to work their way overland to Inverness. However, they were shadowed by patrols of Mackay's – the Mackays were not 'out' in 1745. The next day the small group of Jacobites were confronted by a much larger force of Mackays near Lochan Hakel. There was no escape and no hope, so the few Jacobites began to fling the gold into the lochan. They were soon overpowered, though, and most of the gold was captured and taken on board the *Sheerness*.

Meanwhile, the Prince, desperate for the funds from France, had detached 1,500 of his men, under the command of the Earl of Cromarty, to march north and save the day. They, though, were met and overwhelmed by a joint force led by the Earl of Sutherland and Lord Reay, for few men of the north-east were 'out' in '45. Indeed, not only were they not out, but their chiefs, at least, were positively anti-Jacobite. Those 1,500 Jacobite men were soon to be sadly missed on the field of Culloden, although whether they could have turned the day, or whether they too would lie under those sad cairns on Drummossie Moor is a moot question.

This was not much of a skirmish in terms of warfare, but arguably it sealed the fate of Prince Charles Edward and his foolish, gallant, misguided attempt to gain the crowns of England and Scotland. That little group of Mackays at Lochan Hakel perhaps changed the course of our national history.

Bettyhill is a straggling village amongst barren and rock-strewn moorland, and yet the very name still evokes strong, even violent, feelings amongst Highlanders wherever they are found, from Brisbane to Calgary, from Glasgow to California. This was the place, or one of them, where the crofters settled after being cleared from their land down Strathnaver.

Bettyhill and adjoining Farr could be a Mecca for the archae-ologist, almost as rich as Kilmartin away south-west on the opposite coast. There is an excellent pamphlet, available at the museum, which will direct you to many of the prehistoric remains near the village. If time is pressing, or you are not really greatly interested in historic sites, do at least visit the great burial cairn at Achcoillenaborgie a little south of Bettyhill on the Skelpick road. First used as a burial place perhaps 6,000 years ago, this is a very impressive site indeed, with three burial chambers in a cairn 75 yards long by 15 yards wide. And you can still see the actual burial chambers.

When the Sutherlands of evil memory bought their vast estates in the early years of the 19th century, this was a land of peasant farming, and, by the standards of the day, prosperous enough, and certainly productive. Very large numbers of cattle grazed the hills and straths, with horses and goats and the small native sheep. It was, in fact, mixed farming of a high order.

The hills carried a great variety of rich herbage, manured by cattle and horses for centuries, and the straths were cultivated for corn, and a hay crop was taken. It was a self-sustaining farming system which had long endured, which did not rape the land, and which supported a considerable population.

It would be nonsense to regard the pre-Clearance Highlands as some sort of Arcadia, with merry peasants living a carefree life close to the soil. Indeed, it must have been a hard life, with primitive housing, with periodic hunger and much illness, especially tuberculosis. But it is equally nonsense to regard that life from the standards of today. You must compare the life then with others of the time, with the utter misery and degradation of workers in the new factories and slum cities, with the serf-dom endured by the coalminers and salt workers of Scotland. And when you do that, then perhaps the Highlands were indeed an Arcadia.

There were village schools, and they were well-attended. There were inns and alehouses. And there was a close-knit society with a rich language and culture. Song and poetry and music were the cultural birthright of those peasants, and they were valued.

Of course there were social and economic stresses. When were there not? There were signs of a population explosion, but to a large extent that was being taken care of by voluntary emigration to the New World, where the restless and the foot-itchy saw chances of adventure and riches. There was often hunger at the end of winter for people and animals alike, but famine was unknown. We may look at a carefully preserved 'black house' today, and wonder how human beings could live in such squalor, with their animals sharing the same roof. Well, it certainly is no 'semi' in Surbiton, and there is no wall-to-wall carpet, but we must remember that 150 years ago most of our ancestors lived in such conditions. And lived in infinitely worse conditions if they were fated to be factory workers or slum dwellers in some great city.

The Sutherlands, and many others like them, ended it all, though, Arcadia or not. The misery came to Scotland a hundred years after it had scourged England during the Enclosures in that country, and for the same reasons – of which the chief was greed. In the early 18th century, English society had undergone, with the Enclosures, a degree of misery quite unprecedented, when half the population was below starvation level, when the cities and their factories filled with the cheapest labour fresh from the fields, when the price of a hungry young girl was sixpence, as James Boswell noted.

The same miseries came to Scotland, and frequently from the hands of the same families, families whose wealth was often spent in building great and ostentatious houses in vast parks, lovely and gracious houses we visit today and admire, without a thought of the utter misery and degradation which made such beauty possible.

Then, as still today, a tiny majority of people, many of them strangers, owned most of the land. Today, 0.01% of the population owns two-thirds of the land – 38 individuals own 84% of Sutherland and 76 own 84% of Ross-shire. And this in countryside that is basically agricultural.

The Sutherlands, rich beyond all dreams of avarice, wanted their new estates empty of people, so that sheep could roam everywhere. They wanted the maximum return on their investment, and they employed factors ruthless enough to get it. They were the epitome of Victorian morality and ethics of which we hear so much praise today.

What they introduced was not even good agriculture. The sheep they introduced were the foreign Cheviots, bigger and heavier and more demanding than the small native breeds. They thrived for a while on the stored-up fertility of centuries, then declined, as invariably happens in mono-culture. Rushes, bracken and heather began to flourish where once there had been fertility and they still do.

So the people had to go, by force if necessary, but go they must. Gangs of bully-boys roamed the glens, evicting tenants, burning houses and committing every crime that those with petty power have always committed against a helpless people.

Donald McLeod, who himself suffered eviction, and more than once, wrote of the burning of an isolated homestead near Rossal:

> I was present at the pulling down and burning of the house of William Chisholm, Badinloskin, in which was lying his wife's mother, an old bed-ridden woman of nearly 100 years of age, none of the family being present. I informed the persons about to set fire to the house of this circumstance, and prevailed upon them to wait until Mr. Sellar, the factor, came. On his arrival I told him of the poor old woman being in a condition unfit for removal when he replied 'Damn her, the bitch, she has lived too long — let her burn' Fire was immediately set to the house, and the blankets in which she was carried out were in flames before she could be got out. She was placed in a little shed, and it was with great difficulty they were prevented from firing it also. The old woman's daughter arrived while the house was onfire and assisted the neighbours in removing her mother out

of the flames and smoke, presenting a picture of horror which I shall never forget, but cannot attempt to describe.

So it went on, all over the Highlands and Islands, but nowhere more viciously than here in Sutherland.

And the people were helpless. For centuries they had lived under a patriarchal system that may have been crude and often unjust, but was basically benevolent to the members of the clan. All the people were members of the family of the Clan chief. Now the Clan chiefs had deserted them, had been 'bought by English gold', and the new chiefs had no ear to hear the cries of despair. Even the ministers of the kirk deserted them, advising them that they must obey, that it was their duty to obey their masters, and that their sorrows were punishment for sin.

The factor appointed by the Sutherlands was the notorious Patrick Sellar, a man whose name still stinks in every Highland nostril. He was not only the factor, but a very considerable farmer himself, and grew wealthy – wealthy enough to buy a large estate in distant Morvern, where his first act was to clear off all the tenants.

Before that, though, he farmed in Sutherland. Prior to the Clearances which Sellar organised and conducted, the land Sellar farmed had supported about 2,000 people. When it was a sheep farm, it was worked by just 19 shepherds, all of them brought up from the Borders.

On one occasion in Sutherland, Sellar was charged with the murder of an evicted tenant, and to no-one's surprise, was acquitted by a jury of his peers. Promptly, the sheriff who had had the temerity to charge him was replaced by a more compliant man, a man who was in Sellar's pocket.

Thanks largely to the English newspapers, and not least *The Times* of London, there was a certain amount of outcry about the Clearances, and the estate owners attempted to justify their actions. The Sutherlands actually used Harriet Beecher Stowe's anti-slavery novel *Uncles Tom's Cabin* to provide an apologia for them. She produced a book, now thankfully forgotten, called *Sunny Memories – A visit to Dunrobin.* (Dunrobin was the main seat of the Sutherlands.)

But Donald MacLeod had his answer to her in his Gloomy Memories.

> Had you the opportunity, madam, of seeing the scenes which I and hundreds more have seen – the wild ferocious appearance of the infamous gang who constituted the burning party, their hands and face covered with soot and ashes of the burning houses, cemented by torch-grease and their own sweat, being kept continually drunk or half-drunk while at work; and to observe the hellish amusements some of them would get up too for themselves and for an additional pleasure to their leader... When this fiendish party found any quantity of meal they would carry it to the brink, and dispatch it down the precipice amidst shrieks and yells. It was considered great sport to see the box break to atoms and the meal mixed with the air. When they would set fire to a house, they would watch any of the domestic animals making their escape from the flames, such as dogs, cats, hens or any poultry: these were caught and thrown back to the flames: great sport for demons in human form.

Who was this Donald MacLeod whose pen recorded such

evil? He was a stone mason, born near Rossal in Strathnaver. There was not much work for him locally, and he often travelled to Edinburgh and elsewhere, wherever his work took him. He learned to write English well and fluently, and he was courageous in his opposition to the genocide of his people.

He was, it is perhaps needless to say, a marked man, and was hounded for debts he claimed to have paid in full. In the autumn of 1830, when Donald was working away, his wife and six orphans of the Clearances she was caring for were evicted (for the 13th time!) from their cottage. Eventually, in despair, she set off to walk to distant Thurso, where Donald was working, and she got there, but the experience had unhinged her mind, leaving her, as Donald wrote, 'a living monument of Highland oppression.'

Donald MacLeod emigrated, finally, to Canada, and became a rather unsuccessful bookseller. In 1857 he published his *Gloomy Memories*, a savage and harrowing account of the Clearances, and he challenged the Sutherlands or any of their minions to test his account in court. None did. He died, in some poverty, in 1860, but his book lives, and today there is a memorial to him in Strathnaver, near where he was born.

> In memory of Donald MacLeod
> Stonemason,
> Who witnessed the
> destruction of Rossal in 1814
> and wrote 'Gloomy Memories'.

It is not, of course, an official monument, erected by a grateful government. That seems to be reserved for the Sutherlands and their ilk. It was paid for and erected by local people who are determined that those evils will not be forgotten.

Today, revisionist historians are claiming that the

Clearances were not so vicious as they have been made to appear, and that in any case the Highland economy, society and culture of the pre-Clearance days were obsolescent, that there was growing over-population and extreme poverty and that the Clearances were only a natural progression of a process already happening and inevitable, even beneficial.

As with much revisionist history, it is written for political purposes, and is pernicious nonsense. In truth, the Highlands in those days represented a social and cultural stability of great value and a form of economy flexible enough to have accommodated any changes necessary. Indeed, it is hardly too much to say that one day, and it may be soon, a similar form of tenant farming, with mixed agriculture, will have to be reinstated in the Highlands as the only viable alternative to another Highland Clearance.

If things go on as they are, we can look forward to the day when the few remaining natives will each be dressed by the Tourist Board in a nylon kilt and taught to play *Amazing Grace* on plastic bagpipes for the delectation of visitors.

So what happened to those cleared off their land? Many, and no-one knows how many, were shipped off, voluntarily or not, to the New World, in ships so rotten and overcrowded that they resembled slavers.

Not all who left arrived in the New World: ships were lost at sea. Many were moved to the coasts, and that is why today we see so many crofting villages on the coasts. Those tenant farmers were expected to earn their living by fishing, and the only land they had is what you see today, those pathetic little strips in front of each cottage – cottages which they had to build themselves, and often without the precious roof-timbers which had been burned by the factor and his thugs.

Somewhere around 15,000 people were cleared off the Sutherland estates, and consequently those lovely and once fertile glens

STRATHNAVER MUSEUM

Highland Clearances
Clan Mackay Room
Local History
Farr Stone
Books For Sale

Bettyhill · Sutherland · Tel: (01641) 521418

Open Easter to October
Monday to Saturday
10 a.m.-1p.m./2p.m.-5p.m.

and straths are empty today, and the small population clustered in coastal villages.

Before that short digression on the Clearances, we were at Bettyhill (the Gaelic name is *An Bloran Odor* – The Grey Place.) There are some good beaches near the village at Farr Bay and Torrisdale Bay, and the latter also has a bird sanctuary.

Farr Stone

The Strathnaver Folk Museum is nearby, in an old church, and certainly should be visited, for there is a fine collection of material on the Clearances. It is a community operation, and deserves a good donation. Other local exhibits concern the archaeology and history of the area. The whole effort sprang from the local school and a project done on the Clearances. The results were so impressive that it was decided to make it permanent and expand it.

The justly famous Farr Stone stands in the churchyard. It is an intricately carved cross, with spirals and interlocking incisions. There are two curious birds, perhaps swans, with their necks intertwined, so that each seems to be pecking its own back. It is a glorious piece of Celtic Christian artistry, one of the finest in Scotland, and dates probably from the 9th century. It shows clearly that Celtic Christianity continued to flourish in Sutherland even during the hegemony of the Norsemen. The beauty and intricacy of the carving on the Farr Stone is all the more remarkable when you realise that the artist, a thousand years ago, was not working on a piece of comparatively soft freestone, but on hard and unyielding schist.

From Farr and Bettyhill the road (B871) turns due south for Altnaharra and Lairg. It runs through Strathnaver, the Naver being a salmon river of great fame. It is the river where members of the Royal Family often come to flog the water when they are announced to be 'fishing somewhere in Scotland.'

Strathnaver is pleasant, but quite without the drama and grandeur of the west. Not surprisingly, there are few houses now and no villages along its length. One of those few dwellings is Syre Lodge, to the right of the road half way down the strath, just before a patch of woodland. This was Patrick Sellar's house during the Clearances.

Not far away, and almost opposite Syre Lodge, are the excavated remains of Rossal village, one of the few archaeological sites which allow us to learn more about the life of the Highlands in pre-Clearance days. This was also one of the villages about which Donald MacLeod wrote. Like a thousand other villages, Rossal had been long lost and forgotten when forestry operations began on the site. During the preliminary mapping, the surveyors realised what they had found, and to their eternal credit the Forestry Commission decided to preserve the site.

Archaeological activity was begun, and it was found that there was a township of sixty acres, enclosed by a ring dyke, and by skilled research it was shown that people had lived there since records began in 1269. There are three clusters of houses, each house measuring as much as 108 feet by 12 feet, and there were fifteen families living there when they were evicted and their houses burned in 1830. There were storehouses, barns and byres; it had obviously been a well-settled community.

The remains of the village are well marked and signposted, and give a most unusual insight into a period of recent history that has left few relics.

You will know when you approach Rossal, for one hill top has been left bare of trees. That is it, and there is a marked track from the small carpark. Do please visit it, and give a thought to that little community, inhabited for so long, and so harmless, and yet destroyed in a day to the further glory of Victorian values and morals.

From Syre Lodge and Rossal the road runs along the bank of Loch Naver and to Altnaharra. This is a tiny village, but to the *cognoscenti* is a very famous place for fishing. Apart from that, and possibly as a change if the water is not kind, the village is a splendid centre for touring, and for walking, with some most delightful circular car tours available.

The mountain walking is excellent, with Ben Kilbrech and Ben Hope available for a day in the hills. Ben Hope in particular has a great wealth of alpine flowers, and the walk up its shoulder is invariably a rewarding experience.

There is a long and empty stretch of road between Altnaharra and Lairg, but it is far from boring. The road (A836) offers fine views on both sides, and the hills, lacking perhaps something of the splendour of others in the north, lack nothing in shapeliness and colour. It is a very empty land in all directions, a land of burn and moor and lochan. And yet a bright day in autumn will provide a constantly varied pattern of colour, light and shade that could never pall.

Lairg is the great communication centre for the Highlands, at least by road. Like Rome, all roads lead to it. Little more than a village, though, it has not been spoiled, and the fact that so many roads join there makes it an excellent touring centre.

It lies at the foot of the great Loch Shin, another Mecca for the angler. The salmon heading for Loch Shin must climb the Falls of Shin, a fine torrent pouring through a rocky gorge, and the sight of those great fish leaping up the rapids and struggling to reach their spawning beds after their adventurous double journey across the oceans is not to be missed. There is a viewing platform to let you watch in safety.

A good Forest Walk starts from the carpark at the Falls, and it is well worth doing. The Forestry Commission is to be commended for its (quite recent) policy of laying out such walks, and of providing sufficient and unobtrusive information to make them all the more interesting.

Lairg really comes to life for the sheep sales held every August, for the town is the central market for Sutherland. It has been estimated that a quarter of a million sheep roam the Sutherland glens and hills. In August you could almost swear that they have all been brought to Lairg.

Lairg, like Bettyhill to the north, is a place of great archaeological interest. There are many hut-circles hereabout, and there is a broch at Sullaby. A neolithic cairn, newly excavated, can be inspected at The Ord. The Ord also gives excellent views, making it a good place to visit.

Achany Glen, just to the south, is the site of one of the most fascinating archaeological digs at present going on in Scotland. The area today is a waste of heather and deer grass, but the excavations are revealing human habitation going back to

Neolithic times, and continuing unbroken to the 16th century. It seems that the peace of 2,000 years was broken in 1593, when Ross of Balnagowan raided Achany. There still exists a record of their loot – 50 work horses, 44 mares in foal, 100 cows in calf, 70 oxen, 250 ewes, 200 wedders, 200 she goats and a great wealth of pigs, plaids, wool, weapons, utensils and cash. And all this from land that today carries only a handful of sheep and a few deer!

Just south of Lairg you will see, across the river, a great tur-reted edifice in the worst possible taste, fortunately half hidden by trees today. This is Carbisdale Castle, probably the last castle to be built in Britain. It was put there in 1910, by the Sutherlands, but today it is a Youth Hostel, a fate which seems somehow sin-gularly fitting. But don't sympathise too much with the poor Sutherlands, though, for having to sell off one of their castles. They still own, it has been calculated, over 150,000 acres of the Highlands, and are quite comfortable, thank you.

South of Lairg and you are really out of the Highlands, in a sense, although still well north of Inverness, which likes to be referred to as the Capital of the Highlands. Of course, even south of Inverness you must pass by the Cairngorm, which is the highest mass of land in the whole of Britain, but it is a some-what isolated great plateau, not connected with all the vast empty lands through which we have been travelling for so long.

But before leaving the Highlands altogether, if leave them you must, do make another side trip, this time to Croick Church. You reach it by a side road up Strath Carron from Bonar Bridge, and it is a pleasant little road alongside a sparkling burn.

It was at Croick Church that victims of the Clearances left one of the most poignant records of their misery, for they scratched messages on the window of the church, and you can see them to this day. Having been evicted from the surrounding glens, they sheltered in the churchyard; amongst the messages they scratched was:

> Glen Calvie is a wilderness under sheep... Glen Calvie people was in the churchyard here May 24th 1845... The Glen people was here 1845... The Glen Calvie tenants resided here May 24th 1845... Glen Calvie people the wicked generation... The Glen Calvie tenants resided in the churchyard May 24th 1845.

We will let *The Times* of London have the last word. The Old Thunderer had sent a Special Commissioner (we would call him a correspondent) to report on events in the Highlands, and on Monday June 2nd 1845, that Special Commissioner wrote 'From Ardgay, Near Tain, Ross-shire':

THE CLEARANCES OF THE HIGHLANDERS OF SCOTLAND.

I returned to this place for the purpose of witnessing the sequel to the clearance of the poor Highlanders out of Glen Calvie, an account of which I sent you some days ago. It will be remembered that eighteen poor crofters living in Glen Calvie near here, the legal process for turning them out of their homes having been completed, gave bond peaceably to leave on 24th...

Were any such clearance attempted in England, I leave you to conceive the excitement which it would be certain to create. The mob processions, the effigy burnings, and the window smashings with which every instigator and instrument in so heartless a scene would be reminded that there are principles of action which are thought more honourable, more worthy, and which make living amongst our fellows more pleasant than mere money grubbing.

These poor Highlanders, however, apart from their naturally mild and passive nature, have been so broken in spirit by many such scenes that not a murmur, not a remonstrance escaped them in the completion of this heartless wholesale ejectment. I drove over on Sunday to the Parish Church of Croick, which is near Glen Calvie. Close by a bridge leading to the Glen, the whole of these poor people and the inhabitants of one or two neighbouring straths were assembled to hear one of their elders read the psalms to them. At the Established Church the service was partly in Gaelic and partly in English, and the congregation was miserably thin. Behind the Church in the churchyard a long kind of booth was erected, the roof formed of tarpaulin stretched over poles, the sides closed in with horse cloths, rugs, blankets and plaids. On enquiry, I found that this was the refuge of the Glen Calvie people. They had kept their word and saved their bondsman...

The whole of the people left the Glen, on Saturday afternoon, about 80 in number, and took refuge in this tent erected in their churchyard... I am told it was a most wretched spectacle to see these poor people march out of the glen in a body, two or three carts filled with children, many of them mere infants... A fire was kindled in the churchyard round which the poor children clustered, two cradles with infants were placed close to the fire and sheltered around by the dejected-looking mothers. Others busied themselves in dividing the tent into compartments by means of blankets for the different families. Of the 80 people who passed the night in the churchyard with most insufficient shelter, 23 were children under 10 years of age, 7 persons were sickly and in bad health, and 10 were about 60 years of age. About 8 are young married men. There are a few grown up children and the rest are persons in middle life from 40 to 50...

...Eighteen families of 92 individuals supporting themselves in comparative comfort with not a pauper amongst them. That they owed no rent and were quite prepared to pay as much as anyone in rent for the land which they and their forefathers had occupied for centuries but which it seems is now to be turned into a sheep walk...

It might be wondered why they squatted in the churchyard when there was shelter in the church. The answer is simple: to those God-fearing people it would have been sacrilege to have used their church for anything but worship. So they shivered and suffered outside.

The church itself is interesting, and to those unacquainted with the austerity of Highland religion rather surprising even today. It is stark and simple, inside and out, but very typical of its kind. Built in 1822 with the aid of a government grant, it was to a standardised design by Thomas Telford, who seems to have been responsible for half of the man-made things in the Highlands, and it cost £1,570.

The heap of stones to the west side of the Church is all that remains of a Pictish broch, and that shows for how many centuries man had lived and cultivated these glens before that Great White Plague, the Cheviot sheep, and those who introduced that plague into the glens, drove them away for ever.

CHAPTER 5

Bonar Bridge, Dornoch, Golspie, Dunrobin and Brora

ON THE ROAD NORTH from Ullapool (A835), one has to decide about travelling by the west coast or the east. I am eternally grateful that normally I do not have to make that decision. I travel both ways, and even today could not give any coherent argument for preferring one against the other on any particular day. I think if bad weather is coming in from the south-west, as it sometimes does, then I would head for the east. But if the weather was favouring mists and fog, as is not unknown, I would eschew the east and keep to the west.

Mind you, beautiful and seductive as both are, they are very different. On the west there is the wilderness of great mountains and sea lochs; on the east there are high cliffs and bare moors. If you are wise, you will travel both, but it is certain you cannot travel both, and appreciate both, in one brief holiday. So come back again!

Anyway, the choice has to be made just north of Ullapool. At Ledmore, the A835 joins the A837 its magnificent journey to the north. The smaller, single-track road to the right (the A837) goes gloriously south-east through Glen Oykel and on to Bonar Bridge, for the road north up the rock-bound east coast. For now, we will take the A837.

Loch Borralan is on the right of the road, to the south, and at its eastern end is the Altnacealgach Hotel. That is a Gaelic name, of course, and means something like The Burn of the Deceivers. It is a reminder of the old belief that the men of Ross-shire are deceivers ever. This is just about the old border between Ross-shire and Assynt, and it was fought over and disputed only too often in the old days. In one battle, the men of Ross-shire were adamant that they were standing on the soil of Ross-shire, although clearly they were in Assynt. Being deceivers, they had filled their brogues with soil from their native land, so they were indeed standing (surely very uncomfortably) on the soil of Ross-shire.

Anyway, for their presumption, they lost their heads, but are remembered by the name of the hotel.

Not far past the hotel, a foot-track leads off to the left, over the shoulder of the hill, and across the river Oykel to the very pleasant and lonely Loch Ailsh and Benmore Lodge.

Further along the road again, after some quite dramatic rises and falls, you pass Loch Craggie and run down into Oykel Bridge and Strath Oykel. In the old days, this strath was a major route from east to west of the country and was well populated. Today, like so many others, it is empty of people. The old bridge across the river is closed now, at least to traffic, but it is well worth walking across to look at the gorge just up stream.

About six miles past Oykel Bridge a minor road to the right (there is only one) would lead you in complete solitude for some miles to Invershin and Bonar Bridge. It is a good road, and pleasant travelling, but of course not as fast as the 'improved' main road for Bonar Bridge.

If you continue on that main road, still the A837, and now double-tracked and proud of it, you come to Rosehall and a minor road to the left. This leads for fifteen miles or so back north and west through Glen Cassley, and onto the slopes of Ben More Assynt. It is a dead-end road, but a delightful one, especially near the mouth of the glen, at the Cassley Falls. Here the river has cut its way against the grain of the rocks, and has left a strange, almost lunar, landscape. Travel that road, right to its end amongst the peat hags and lochans of Ben More Assynt. There is no quieter road in all of Scotland.

There is a road junction on the main road not far from the mouth of Glen Cassley, at Rosehall. The A839 bears off left to Lairg, and the A837 continues to the right towards Invershin and Bonar Bridge. It is the A837 we shall travel. If you take the other road, to Lairg, you can go north and east through Strath Fleet and on to Golspsie, but in doing that you would miss the charming road along the north side of the Dornoch Firth, and also miss the town of Dornoch, which would be a great pity.

Bonar Bridge is a road junction, and until recently was a busy place. It is easily seen from quite a distance, because the girders of the bridge itself rear up in a way that justify its name – the Coathanger. But at least the bridge is there and doing its job, which is more than you can say for the first bridge to be built there, by Thomas Telford. It was swept away in a great flood, and the second bridge did not last long either. You can read about them both on a plaque beside the present bridge.

Bonar Bridge is no longer such a busy road junction as it was in the past, because a great new bridge has been built across the Dornoch Firth which carries the main road north without the long detour to the head of the Firth. That completes the bridging of the three great firths north of Inverness – the Moray, the Cromarty and the Dornoch. In days not so long ago, ferries transported carriages and passengers across these firths, and across the mouth of Loch Fleet, and not only were the ferries an expensive hindrance to travel, but they were also dangerous, and many lives were lost there. In one disaster, the ferry crossing the Dornoch Firth overturned, and almost one hundred lives were lost. That was in August 1809, and the travellers were headed for the great Lammas Fair at Tain.

The road from Bonar Bridge to Dornoch is delightful, and is even better now that the new bridge is opened, and all the heavy traffic bound for the north goes that way, leaving the old road to be enjoyed by those who take their pleasure by meandering along wooded byways, through well-farmed land along the side of a sea-loch. In truth, is was never a busy road, by modern standards, but it is even better now that is has become a minor spur.

About three miles from Bonar Bridge you will pass the rounded hill of Dun Creich. The 'Dun' indicates a fort, and that hill is crowned by what was once a truly massive vitrified fort, the most northerly in Scotland. It covers about one and a half acres on the top of the hill, and, like all vitrified forts, dates from the Iron Age. Naturally, after so many hundreds of years, there is not a lot of it left now, but the inner and outer ramparts can still be traced. Standing on the hill top, you get a very clear impression of just how impregnable it must have been once, and how intimidating.

At Spinningdale a minor road comes in to join the A949. This is an alternative route from Bonar Bridge, and it is a pleasant and interesting road, running past Loch Migdale. The Bonar Bridge golf course is there, and it would be a grand course to play, so long as you managed to concentrate on the game, and not on the delightful vista of moors and loch. Some Bronze Age tragedy, of which we shall never know the details, once took place near here, for a wonderful hoard of relics was found, sheets of bronze, an axe, armlets, beads and buttons. It was a whole treasure, almost certainly carefully buried in some time of trouble, and then lost for about 2,000 years until its recent chance discovery.

Incidentally, you can, if you so wish, take the same minor road all the way north and east to the shores of Loch Fleet, near Golspie. It is a fine and interesting road, lonely, and running through high moors, past high mountains and lochs. Travel it if you can, but not at the expense of missing Dornoch.

Spinningdale, on the A949, is a place one would normally drive straight through and hardly notice. Down by the shore, though, are the gaunt ruins of an old cotton mill, and the unusual, English-sounding name came from that.

The mill was built in 1790 by David Dale, the leading cotton manufacturer in the country, and incidentally the father-in-law of Robert Owen. It was a five-storey building, with Palladian windows, and is still impressive in its ruination. It started with a hundred workers, but was never a financial success, chiefly because of its remoteness from markets. A fire destroyed the building in 1808, and it has been a ruin ever since. It is a pity, perhaps, that Robert Owen never got to Spinningdale and transformed it, as he did New Lanark into his vision of an ideal industrial community.

The owner of the mill was George Dempster of Skibo, one of the better and more far-sighted of the 'improving' landlords of his day. He bought the estate in 1786, and ran it until his death, at the age of 86, in 1818. He had been held in real affection by all his tenants, and not surprisingly, for he did not share the common landlords' view that large sheep-runs were the best and most profitable use of land. Instead, he encouraged his tenants to stay, and even gave them life-leases instead of the normal short lease, or even no lease.

In fact, George Dempster was a remarkable man, and surely should be better known and honoured. He worked with the East India Company, but left after bitter quarrels over his insistence that Indians should be given a share of management, and it was then that he bought Skibo. His major interest at that time was the promotion of a society to extend and protect the fishing industry. The company was well financed by Dempster and others, and built harbours and quays on land they bought. In particular, George Dempster was interested in encouraging the export of salmon, packed in ice, for the London market.

Even today you can see the icehouses he had built in several of the fishing harbours along this coast.

As the owner of the large Skibo estate, of course, he had many, almost feudal, rights over his lands and 'his' tenants. He resigned most of those rights, and allowed the others to fall into disuse. He was a great one for draining land, and by that, and by the use of large deposits of fertilising marl, he vastly improved the fertility of the Skibo estate. It was unfortunate that the war with France, when it began in 1793, wrecked all Dempster's plans for Scottish fishing, and doubly unfortunate that such a reasonable and progressive man should have been in such close proximity to the arrant Countess of Sutherland, for she gave all Scottish landowners a bad name.

Skibo Castle, where George Dempster lived, lies between the road (A949) and the sea, just by Clashmore. You can't see anything of it from the road, and it is in private hands, so you cannot visit unless you are a member of the exclusive Carnegie Club. There is little left of the original, for each owner seems to have been one of those who fall in love with a house, buy it, and then proceed to change it completely. In the Middle Ages it was a residence of the Bishops of Dornoch, but was much changed by others such as George Dempster.

It was Andrew Carnegie, though, who wrought the biggest changes. Carnegie was the very epitome of the Scotsman on the make. He was born in a poor family in Dunfermline, and went as a youth to America as a poor emigrant. There he flourished, and by means not always ethical, acquired ownership of a large part of the American steel industry. His fortune was enormous and his income equally so – in 1900 he declared an income of 23 million dollars. Carnegie never forgot his Scottish roots, and perhaps also some of the lessons he learned in the kirk at Dunfermline. His great wealth was equalled by his great philanthropy – which of course was never extended to the workers in his own plants. But many a Scottish town still boasts a Carnegie library or Institute, set up and paid for by Andrew Carnegie.

When he bought Skibo Castle he built an extension bigger than the original building, and turned it all into a very lavish mansion, with a nine-hole golf course in the grounds. He was no absentee landlord, and spent four or five months there every year, entertaining very lavishly many people prominent in the arts and politics, and even King Edward VII.

Andrew, who was born in 1835, died in 1918, but his daughter continued the tradition of annual visits. That daughter was aged two when she laid the foundation stone for the extension to Skibo Castle, and her father was then sixty-four. She died in 1990, aged ninety-three. Until the last, the old lady continued her interest in and support for whatever she saw as being beneficial to the people of Dornoch and district.

One of the strangest legends of this north country is connected with the stretch of road between Clashmore and Dornoch. If you turn right off the A949 at Clashmore, and head south towards the Firth (incidentally getting the best view of Skibo Castle) you come to Meikle Ferry, which was the northern end of the old ferry across the Firth. It is a fine and quiet place today, with a view across the Firth to where a long sandy spit of land, the southern terminus of the ferry, reaches out across the water.

On the road between Meikle Ferry and Dornoch you will find a farm called Cyderhall. That is how the name has evolved over centuries, but originally it was *Sigurd's Howe* – the mound of Sigurd – and it was there that Sigurd was buried in the ninth century.

Sigurd was a Norseman, one of those rampaging and ravening types who came each year in their fearful longships, across the grey waters from Norway to Scotland, and far beyond. Sigurd was special, though, for he was the Earl of Orkney, no less, and one of the leaders of the Norse attempt to occupy Caithness. They succeeded, too, and the whole north of Scotland, Caithness, Sutherland, and as far south as Strath Oykel, were Norse possessions. It was not all peaceful, though, particularly on the borders of the Norse lands, where the native peoples still struggled hard to drive the invaders out.

One of the leaders of the resistance on that southern border was a Mormaor or chief called Maelbrigte. He was a brave man and a stout fighter, but he was best known for having very prominent buck teeth. Brave though he was, and stout though he was, when Sigurd and he met in battle, Maelbrigte fell, and in triumph Sigurd cut off his head, and rode off with that trophy tied to his saddle. Perhaps Sigurd had his mind on more plunder, or perhaps just on a mug of mead and a warm fireside. He certainly was not thinking about Maelbrigte, whose head was bouncing up and down beside his leg, tied by the long hair to the saddle-horn. Sigurd did not even notice that Maelbrigte's long buck teeth had scratched his leg as the head bounced around.

It was not long after that, though, that Sigurd was laid low, and died, from a poisoned leg. Maelbrigte had his revenge. One has to wonder what on earth Maelbrigte had eaten to make his teeth so deadly poisonous! Anyway, Sigurd was buried in Sigurd's Howe, and that has changed over the centuries to Cyderhall.

Just along the road is Dornoch, one of Scotland's most delightful small towns. Dornoch is fortunate in that the main road does not pass through the town, and so the roaring and hammering of heavy traffic is blissfully absent. Dornoch is the kind of town where you can stand and blether in the middle of the square, and the few vehicles will drive round you, not over you.

Dornoch has a long history, and not a peaceful one. The

powerful families of Sinclair, MacKay and Murray have seen to that, as they roistered and fought down the centuries.

The first records show that St Barr or Finbarr had a chapel there in the sixth century – its site is marked at the east end of the churchyard. St Barr, of course, belonged to that great out-pouring of saintly missionaries which so distinguished the Celtic church. They came from Iona and Lindisfarne, and spread their beliefs not only over Scotland but also to much of Europe, until they and their beliefs and their asceticism collided with the different beliefs and practices of the Roman church. The simplicities of the Celtic church could not survive the opposi-tion of the powerful and centralised church of Rome, and it vanished. Just the same, it is not too fanciful to imagine that some of the austerities of the Scottish kirk owe something to the ancient inheritance of the Celtic saints, as well as to the asceticism of John Knox.

The cathedral of Dornoch was founded by Gilbert de Moravia, the fourth bishop, and the first cathedral charter appears to have been about 1224. There is a copy (in Latin, of course) on the wall in the transept, and it laments that there was only one priest, and that this was a place of poverty, and the scene of frequent invasions. Gilbert appears to have been an efficient administrator, as well as being somewhat dictatorial. He instructed that all fourteen parishes in his diocese should contribute to the upkeep of the cathedral, and stipulated just how long each year each appointed priest must stay at Dornoch.

The cathedral has had a hard life, but somehow has sur-vived both destruction and almost disastrous renovation. There is still much remaining of the original fabric, done in the best Transitional style. The pillars and arches, the tower and the choir are all original.

Some of the stained glass is interesting, especially perhaps the Carnegie windows on the north side of the chancel. The three windows specifically remind us of how Andrew Carnegie gave away his wealth. The one nearest the communion table reminds us that he built the Carnegie Hall in New York and was a founder of the Pittsburgh Philharmonic Orchestra. He also donated more than 7,000 organs to churches around the world; the central figure in the window holds a set of organ pipes. The middle window reminds us that Carnegie gave much wealth to promote the cause of peace between nations, and that the outbreak of war in 1914 almost broke his heart. It was he who financed the rather ludicrous Peace Palace in The Hague. The third window reminds us that Carnegie donated and financed more than 3,000 libraries throughout the world, and endowed many University scholarships.

For me, though, the most pleasing windows are those in the south porch, which depict the flora and fauna of the Highlands, and are quite delightful. The one facing east shows its full colour in winter and in the evenings. It is inspired by a Highland gloaming and heralds the magical time between sunset and star shine. Quite delectable.

Other things of beauty are the tapestries in the choir and the elders' seats. These again depict the birds and the wild flowers of Sutherland.

As was noted earlier, the cathedral has survived both destruction and restoration. The destruction occurred in 1570 when a complicated three-way struggle for power between Sinclairs, McKays and Murrays resulted in the Sinclair men burning the cathedral and taking away everything they could lift. They even broke open the tomb of Bishop Gilbert in their search for loot, although it is said that the Sinclair who kicked the tomb open very soon afterwards contracted some fearful disease in that foot, and died of it.

The building remained roofless for many years, until in

1616 a new roof was put over the choir and the transept, and that area became the parish kirk. It was not until 1835 that the rest of the building was re-roofed and restored, under the patronage of the Countess of Sutherland. Whoever chose the architect William Burn to do the job must have been handicapped by a total lack of sensibility. Burn had just completed the 'restoration' of St Giles in Edinburgh, and had managed virtually to destroy its dignity and beauty. He did not do quite so well in Dornoch.

Fortunately for us today, a restoration of the restoration was done in 1924, and at least some of the original austerity is to be seen again.

Dornoch is much more than its cathedral, though, even though the cathedral is most certainly a place to be visited and appreciated.

Just across the green from the cathedral is the hotel which was once the Bishops' Palace. Built in the sixteenth century, it still presents its old facade to the public, and the modern bits are well hidden.

Dornoch, of course, is the Royal Burgh of Dornoch, an honour bestowed on the town by Charles 1 in 1628. That was rather ironical, in a way, for the next time the town suffered the depredations of a marauding army, they were those of General Middleton, Charles 11's commander-in-chief in Scotland.

At the time of the Restoration, Middleton and his men landed at Little Ferry on Loch Fleet, and made their headquarters at Dornoch, the Royal, and previously loyal, Burgh. They were joined there by allies, including the Chief of MacKay. However, when Cromwell's army marched north to engage them, Middleton withdrew without waiting for battle, and the McKays took yet another opportunity (they never missed one) to pillage and loot the town and the cathedral.

The Town Jail, in the handsome set of buildings next to the

Castle Hotel, facing the Cathedral, is interesting, but not nearly as interesting as it would have been if modern vandals had not been at work. Part of the jail was used as a military prison for a hundred years, and in their inimitable way, those generations of Jocks from every Scottish regiment have left records of their stay scratched on the walls of the cells. They must have been a fascinating comment on the lives and sorrows and hopes of those men, but all have been obliterated behind new plaster and white-wash.

You will see the seal of the Royal Burgh here and there in the buildings, and please note that in the centre is a horse shoe. It is said that this commemorates a battle in 1259, when the Norsemen landed at nearby Skibo, and William, the first Earl of Sutherland led the defending army. He lost his sword in the fray, but seized the first weapon he could, which happened to be the severed leg of a horse, and used that to lay about him so vigorously that the Norsemen fled the field. You can believe it if you like.

ROVIE FARM GUEST HOUSE
Rogart, Sutherland IV28 3TZ.
Tel: 01408 641209

Rovie Farm Guest House is a commodious lodge-style farmhouse in picturesque Strathfleet, just 4 miles off the A9 on the A839 Mound-Lairg road. This is a beef and sheep working farm.

Our aim to is provide Highland hospitality at its best, with 'home from home' facilities. There is good home cooking, and all rooms have every comfort. There is a residents' lounge and separate dining and T.V. room.

A holiday at Rovie Farm can be one of total relaxation or of strenuous exercise, just as you wish. Fishing, swimming, golf, pony trekking, and lovely walks – they are all there for your delight. There are innumerable sites of architectural and historical interest.

A quite delightful Victorian drinking fountain stands in front of the cathedral. It is cast iron, and very elaborate, complete with the arms of Sutherland. There are also some crocodiles, yes crocodiles, cast in there somewhere, for some reason, and you are challenged to find them.

There is much more to Dornoch than the Cathedral and the town centre, of course. There is golf, for one thing. It is played on the links of the Royal Dornoch Golf Club, and a superlatively fine course it is. It is 'Royal' because Edward VII played there, but more interestingly, the history of the course goes back to the early seventeenth century.

Another thing which distinguishes Dornoch is the many miles of beach and the great wealth of sea birds. There is no limit to the highly pleasurable walking you can do from Dornoch, both seashore and country.

But even Dornoch cannot hold us indefinitely, and we must resume our journey to the far north. You can, if you wish, go on the minor road past Embo and see 'Grannie's Heilan Hame' and its associated caravan complex. Personally, I would go back to the main road, the A9, by the short cut of the B9168. You pass the town cemetery, where a large sign forbids overnight parking!

Skelbo castle is close by, but not easy to find, in spite of signs. It is a very old castle, and little remains of it today, just a few battered stone walls on top of a wooded mound. That mound may well be the remains of a Norman motte-and-bailey castle, itself replaced, probably in the fourteenth century, by what we see today.

Nothing much ever happened at Skelbo, but it was there that the emissaries of Edward I of England stopped when they travelled north to meet the Maid of Norway. They intended to escort her to London, and marry her to the King's son. She was the Queen of Scots by birth, and would be the Queen of

England by marriage, and as the only child of her father, could have been Queen of Norway. She was seven years old, and the lad she was to marry was only six.

But it was not to be. Seven hundred years ago, the ship carrying the Maid ventured out into the wild and tempestuous waters of the autumn gales. Somewhere on the journey, perhaps at Kirkwall, the little girl died, and the dynastic dreams of Edward I suffered a sad blow. What he could not have by deception he tried to gain by force, and the long series of wars between England and Scotland began.

The Maid's mother was Margaret, Queen of Norway, and the only child of Alexander III of Scotland. He was a good King, who reigned over what was known as Scotland's Golden Age. It was an unmitigated tragedy when he died one stormy night as he rode from Edinburgh to join his wife. He and three others crossed the Queen's Ferry, but somewhere in the blackness of that night, before they reached Kinghorn, the King's horse stumbled, and he was killed, incidentally fulfilling the dire prophesies made at his wedding feast by Thomas the Rhymer.

There is no ferry crossing Loch Fleet now. Instead, there is the remarkable Mound. This is a great earthen embankment, faced with stone on the seaward side, which keeps the sea from sweeping far up the valley of the river Fleet. By stopping the tide, many acres of good valley-bottom land have been brought into cultivation. But the Mound is much more than just a dyke against the sea. There had to be provision for the river to flow through it, and for fish, especially salmon, to get upstream. It was Thomas Telford who designed and built the Mound, and devised the great wooden valves which close automatically against the sea and open automatically to let the river flow.

So much in the Highlands was designed and built by Telford that it is easy to take him for granted. That would be a mistake, for we owe much to him, and his skills, and what seemed to be his innate good taste. He was incapable of building an ugly structure. If only just a little of his genius had been inherited by the architects of today!

In any case, he was responsible for the Mound, although two extra arches had to be added in 1837, and it was completed on June 26th, 1816, when the Countess of Sutherland was the first to cross.

Much of Loch Fleet and the land to the west of the Mound is now a nature reserve, and its special feature is the bird life which congregates there, both along the shores and in the large natural growths of woodland.

It is just by the Mound that the other road, the minor road, from Bonar Bridge, joins the main A9 road north. Another road, the A839 also comes in from the west, from Lairg and joins the A9 just by the Mound. From there to Golspie is but a step.

Golspie is really a town, and quite a busy one, but attractive with it, and determined to keep its reputation. Thrice Golspie has been selected as the best-kept place in the north of Scotland.

This was and is the centre of power for the Sutherland family, and you can't escape it. There is that sense of dependency on the great family, and constant reminders of their generosity and kindliness – or at least that is what most of the residents say. There is the same feeling in Inveraray, way off to the west, where the Campbells hold sway, and also south at Glamis.

Not that the Sutherlands can ever let you forget their dominance. It is stamped on the town by the vast statue on the top of Beinn a'Bragaidh. This figure of the first Duke of Sutherland stands thirty feet high on a great column of stone, and can be seen for miles around. There is no road up to it, and the track is steep, but if you do go there you will fnd a typically nauseating and canting inscription to the man who was ...*a judicious, kind and liberal landlord, who identified the improvement of his vast estates with the prosperity of all who cultivated them.* It seems that this paragon would open his hands to the distress of the widow, the sick and the traveller. In deep-cut capital letters it emphasises that *A MOURNING AND GRATEFUL TEN-ANTRY, UNITING WITH THE INHABITANTS OF THE NEIGHBOURHOOD, ERECTED THIS PILLAR, AD 1834.*

To fully appreciate the irony of this, you will understand that this was the very man who, with his wife, had authorised the clearance of all tenants from the glens and straths.

Dunrobin Castle is in a superb cliff-top position, and offers great views from some of the windows. The name, of course, means 'The Fort of Robin', and that was the sixth Earl, who died in 1427. Parts of his old fort can still be picked out in the structure of the modern castle, and you can recognise them by the reddish stone and the comparative coarseness of the work.

It would be tedious to relate the history of the Sutherlands. Suffice it to note that it contained perhaps more than the usual share of treachery, deceit, greed and deception. There is quite enough of those in all Highland history, and it can be no surprise that this particular family participated.

It is surprising, though, to find the interior of the Castle in such appallingly bad taste. In most castles some interior decorator has been employed, and has given at least some semblance of elegance. In other cases artists of the stature of Robert Adam, even, have been employed to produce Highland Castles of dignity and even beauty. They have failed at Dunrobin.

The exterior of the castle is hardly attractive, since the mid-nineteenth century architect Sir Charles Berry modelled it on a Loire Chateau. It is incongruous to have a fairy-tale castle on that stern coast. Berry had just finished building the Houses of Parliament when he received his commission from the Sutherlands, and perhaps he was suffering from an attack of the grandeurs.

Inside, not content with the usual Highland stag heads, the

Sutherlands also have tiger and lion skins – no less than five tiger skins covering the billiard table alone. There is a handful of decent pictures, and one especially fine Canaletto, but the one real reason for visiting Dunrobin must be to look out over the gardens to the sea. The view from the drawing room windows is fine indeed, and better than you get from the gardens themselves.

The other reason, of course, is the museum. The Sutherlands have not left much in the way of historical remains untouched on their lands, and the collection of generations is there in the museum. The Pictish stones are particularly interesting. The oldest, a symbol-stone, dates back perhaps to the seventh century. These symbol-stones are still a complete puzzle, as indeed the Picts are generally. The symbol-stones are unworked slabs or boulders on which are incised various symbols, which to us appear to be such things as mirrors,

Pictish decorations from stone carvings

95

combs, bears and eagles, as well as strange designs and fantasy animals. Later, as Christianity gained ground, the symbol of a cross appeared, not replacing, but complementing, the ancient symbols.

You will find several such stones at Dunrobin, and much else of interest, although perhaps the emphasis on big-game hunting is a little excessive, especially after seeing the tiger skins used as rugs in the library.

If you are staying at Golspie (and it is a good place to stay) there are a number of walks of great interest. The first, which gives truly spectacular views along the coast and out to sea is up Beinn a'Bragaidh – your map might have this Englished to 'Ben Braggie'. That is the hill on which the Duke of Sutherland's statue stands. If you start at the Fountain Road car park, walk along past the fountain, enjoying the lovely old sandstone houses, and go under the railway bridge. Bear left at the fork in the road and follow the track to another fork when you bear left again to a a narrow path on the right, leading to a forestry track and the signposted route up past peat bogs to the summit. Enjoy the 1300 feet climb.

Today you will no longer see the graffiti which once, it is said, decorated the Sutherland column:

There once was a grand Duke of Sutherland,
Whose crofters were fond of their motherland,
But to each one he said,
Your passage is paid,
And off you must go to some other land.

Instead, enjoy the view over the one million or so acres to which the Sutherlands laid claim.

The Big Burn at Golspie is only 5 miles long from its source in Loch Forlary, but some of its short length is through a delightful gorge, with rapids and waterfalls, and it gives the impression of being a much greater river than it really is. You can walk along its length, following the track up the side of the burn from beside the Sutherland Arms Hotel. It is a very pleasant after-dinner stroll.

Another nice little stroll from Golspie is down the narrow road to Little Ferry. There are a few places where you can safely leave a car on the road, and then walk through the wood and along the shore. There is a plethora of unusual and lovely plants, and of course the bird life along the shore is constantly entertaining.

Back on the road (and it is still the A9), just a couple of miles north of Golspie there is the ruin of a broch known locally as a 'Pict's Hoose'. I have described earlier in this book how the brochs were constructed, and mentioned the sense of awe they inspire. This one just north of Golspie, known as Carn Liath, is not much more than waist-high now, but you can clearly see the elaborate double-skin construction.

It is right by the road side, and there is a convenient car park on the opposite side of the road, with a track leading to the ruin. It is a pity that visitors have left so much detritus in the way of soft-drinks cans and plastic wrappers, but at least they have not littered the broch.

Of course, instead of following this main road north from Golspie, there is a very attractive alternative, if you are not in a hurry, and no-one should be in a hurry when visiting the north of Scotland. Take the minor road to the left in Golspie, and go off into the hills, along the Golspie Burn and under the shoulder of Ben Horn. Keep turning and bearing right all the way, and you will make a great circle through the hills and then run down the length of Loch Brora and into the village of Brora. It is a very good diversion for the Highland Wanderer. At one point on that road a track (it is little more) dives off to the left for Ben Armine Lodge, about six miles away. And six delectable miles they are, for the walker who can appreciate total solitude, hill lochs and burns, and the company of all the birds of the moorland. You will walk back the same way, but that track is delightful either way.

Brora, the next town north, gets its name from the Norse for 'River of the Bridge', and not so long ago this was the site of the only bridge in Sutherland.

By now we are well in the country influenced, indeed, controlled, for so long by the Norsemen. It was in 875 AD that the Vikings came to Caithness. Thorstein the Red, allied to the Earl of Orkney, landed and swept down through the whole of Caithness and far south. They held control for the next 400 years. We tend to think indeed, we have long been taught, that the Vikings came only as raiders and plunderers, and that, having wreaked their wicked will, they sailed off home again.

That in fact was not so. The majority of the Norsemen were peaceful farmers and fisherfolk. The pillaging and raiding was the summer activity of the nobility, who of course demanded that the peaceful farmers leave their ploughs and take up their swords. They were a hard bunch with hard names, and we know a lot of them through the Sagas, which sing only of the raids and the victories, not of the peaceful settlements. It is only in recent years with the excavations at such places as York and Whithorn, on the Solway, that we have learned of the vast trading centres and other permanent Norse establishments in Britain.

The sagas tell us of Einar the One-Eyed, Havard Season Prosperous, Einor Butter-Bread, Einor HardJaw, Haliden Longleg, and many others, but they say nothing about the many thousands of immigrants who settled permanently on these shores and wrought a living and lived in peace.

It all ended in 1263, for in that year the Norse finally

conceded that their sovereignty did not extend to the mainland. The Norse king, Hakon, sought to make clear his command, and sailed with a great fleet to Orkney, and then on to Caithness, levying taxes and exacting tribute. He then sailed to Mull and Kintyre, to meet defeat at the hands of the Scottish king at Troon. He retreated, for the last time, and the following year the Scottish Crown levied the taxes in Caithness.

Unlike the Picts, whom they replaced, the Norse have left us plenty of evidence of what they did and how they lived. Indeed, out of all the peoples who have lived in Scotland, only the Picts are silent, and we puzzle over their lovely stone carvings, and their strange Ogam script, and understand not a word of it.

There were three classes of Norsemen. There was the aristocracy, the Earls and their immediate family and followers. They lived in large houses hung with tapestries. They drank wine and mead, played chess, and listened to bards and harpers. They were the leaders in battle and the captains of those lovely long-ships. The ships were strong, but flexible, the better to face the breaking grey Northern seas they

sailed. They were armoured by the blacksmiths, men who had a very special place of high honour in the community. It was the blacksmiths who knew the secrets of making those great elaborately-decorated broadswords and curved axes, the main weapons of the warriors, who so revered their arms that they were buried with them.

Below the aristocrats were the freemen, the smallholders. They had some land, and they raised cattle, sheep, pigs and horses, and grew scant crops of rye, oats and barley, and fished the shallow seas. But when the Earl called, they put off their farming clothes and donned the helmets and leather jerkins of warriors, for they were the men who had to do the fighting when the Earl felt the sap rising in his veins each summer.

Below them again were the bondsmen, the thralls, little better than slaves. Killing them was no great crime, but they were useful for tilling the fields or pulling an oar, and sometimes one of their girl-children would take the fancy of a warrior or even an Earl's son.

CHAPTER 6

Brora, Helmsdale, Berriedale and Dunbeath

SO, WE HAVE REACHED Brora. It is not the town it used to be, for, almost incredibly, Brora used to be a centre of industrialisation in an area of agriculture and fishing. Even more incredibly, Brora was a coalmining town, and had been since 1598. The mine closed in the early 1970s, but maybe not for good, because surveys have shown deposits of more than eight million tons of coal, and the day is surely coming when Scotland's vast reserves of coal will again have to be exploited to replace, to some little extent, the squandered oil of the late 20th century.

The presence of coal attracted other industries, particularly salt-pans and brickmaking, both of which used the local coal to good advantage. The engineering shed, used when a railway was laid from the coalmines to the new harbour, was converted to a weaving shed, and it is still that. The Clynelish Distillery was set up in 1819 (again, of course, like everything else, by the Duke of Sutherland) to use both his coal and the greatly increased corn harvests from his lands. The distillery is still there, and still produces a very palatable full-flavoured malt whisky.

Beyond Brora, the road, now running north-east, begins to go through changing country. The hills are closer to the sea, and the road and railway must stay close together, running for a long way on a raised beach. There are fewer trees, and the bare hills begin to get that skinned, almost skeletal, look of the far north. There are many miles of sandy beaches, a haven for countless sea birds.

The next town north is Helmsdale, and that is one place you really should not pass through without stopping. Apart from anything else, Helmsdale is an attractive town, in an attractive position, but it also houses a very fine exhibition, which they call Timespan. This is an extra-ordinarily well-done evocation of the past, which manages to evade the temptation to be either academic or patronising. Most of all, it is free of the pernicious, tartanised romanticism of some other exhibitions.

Timespan is a highly professional, beautifully organised, journey introducing Highland heritage. I don't want to spoil it for anyone by describing it in detail, but I do want to make it clear that all visitors to the north should devote a couple of hours to this exhibition. You will have a much greater understanding of the country and the people at the end of it.

Helmsdale is the 'Hjalmundsdalr' of the Icelandic sagas, the valley of Hjalmund, and it is now, and always has been, an important centre. A great strath sweeps from Helmsdale right through the wild country to the north coast. The Helmsdale river runs through it, and it has always been a great highway. It still is, although you would hardly think so as you drive its miles of solitude, with hardly another vehicle for ten miles.

Helmsdale was also one of the major herring fishing harbours, another trade that has virtually gone from Scotland. The first curing station was built (by the Sutherlands, of course) in 1814, and John Rennie designed the harbour. A new planned village was established, and soon filled up with crofters forced off their land. In 1818, the new harbour was finished, and from curing 5,000 barrels, the village turned out 46,571 barrels of herring in 1839.

That was typical of the great herring boom, when men went down to the sea and brought back millions of the silver darlings, and saw them gutted, salted and packed in barrels for export to half the world, wherever the fleshy, oily Caithness herring was appreciated. Perhaps 100 million fish were brought ashore every season, and the economy of Scotland was transformed.

It was not just employment for the men, but the women too. The fisher lasses had their jobs to do, and they travelled from west to east, from north to as far south as Hull and Grimsby each year, as the shoals moved down the coast.

And what shoals they were! They were so dense in the water that the sea became oily and silvery when they rose to eat. They had long been caught on lines and used as bait for cod; now they were fished, and fished, and fished again, by the latest devices, by drift nets a mile long, and by steam drifters, and gradually the shoals disappeared. A hundred explanations were given for that disappearance, everything from the wrath of God to some mysterious cycle of breeding. Few listened to the voices which spoke of over-fishing almost to the point of extinction.

There are still herring out there under the cold grey sea, but not many of them, and never again will you walk dryshod across the harbours, where the boats were once bunched so tightly. Never again will the fisher lasses rise from their bunks at dawn, wrap their raw-chapped hands in old rags, and go to the gutting sheds, where their knives would flash, almost too fast to follow, as the harvest of the night was beheaded and gutted and thrown to the packers.

Before the death of the industry, though, in the mid-nineteenth century, about two hundred boats fished out of Helmsdale alone, and the harbour had been twice extended. When the herring declined, there was fishing for white fish, but that could never take the place of the herring, and quite quickly, as quickly as it had grown, Helmsdale lost its fishing industry.

Our road north all the way from Golspie has been parallelled by the railway. If you have travelled from Bonar Bridge north to Lairg and then to Golspie, the road and railway have been companionably close all the way. Helmsdale was the end of the line until 1870. The great empty region to the north and east still relied on horses and feet, and of course, sail, for all its communications. But there was great demand to open up that territory. Shooting, fishing and aping the supposed way of life of Highland Chieftains was the great desire of many newly-rich families in England. The Balmoralisation of the Highlands had begun, thanks largely to the infatuation of Queen Victoria and Albert with things supposedly Scottish. So the railway had to go north, up to Wick and to Thurso. The route was obvious. Not up the coast anymore, for the coast was high cliffs, with great gashes here and there where rivers poured down. Strath Kildonan, or, properly, Strath Ullie, leads north from Helmsdale, with the river Helmsdale flowing through it, rich with salmon, and tempting to the weary owners of England's booming manufactures.

So the railway was driven up there, and then east over the moors to Wick and north to Thurso. It had all seemed easy enough when the Board met for the first time – in Dunrobin Castle, of course. There were sixty miles of track to be laid between Helmsdale (actually, it was fifty-nine miles, one furlong and two and three quarter chains), and it was not easy. Much of the route was peat-bog, and the amount of cutting and filling and ballasting was enormous. As the work progressed, out of the strath and over the moors, many tons of rock had to be shifted.

The workers were the usual itinerant labourers, the navvies who had built everything from canals to tunnels to railways to roads. They would, and did, move mountains, drain seas and block rivers. They lived rough and hard, in isolated camps, and were resented wherever they went. Those navvies were the truly unsung heroes of Britain's industrial expansion, and they have never received the recognition they should have. Only Pat McGill, in his handful of novels, has given them some measure of recognition, and that was because he had been a navvy himself.

Building the Wick railway was a tough one, even for those men. The wooden huts provided for their accommodation could not keep out the rain and frost and snow of those winters, and many fell ill with chest complaints and dysentery. They were snowed in. They ploutered in waist-deep mud and wet peat. They baked under the June sun and only the horses had a worse time of it. But the track-laying went on, and on 9th June 1874, the Duke of Sutherland drove his own engine and carriage the seventy-five miles from Dunrobin to Wick in four and half hours. Civilisation had come to the north.

Another aspect of the 'civilising' of the north is to be found at Helmsdale. Just south of the town itself are the districts of West Helmsdale and Gartymore. At a good view point there, at a bridge over the burn, a pillar bears a plaque reading:

In Memory of the Highland Heroes of the Land League.
They laid the Foundation that we might build thereon.
Gartymore 1881-1981.

This is a poignant reminder of the great struggles waged by the crofters towards the end of last century to get some sort of security and formal tenancy.

The history is too long and complicated to relate here, and

for an understanding of it you should go to one of several books, such as *The Crofting Years* by Francis Thompson. In essence, though, the crofters were threatened with dispossession from the lands they cultivated. These were the descendants of the very people who had been driven from their land fifty years earlier during the Clearances. They had settled where they could, usually on land so barren than even the landlords could think of no use for it. There they had quite literally made soil for their fields, carrying shell sand and seawrack from the shores and placing it carefully wherever they found somewhere free of rocks. They had learned to make some sort of living from whatever was left to them.

Now the landlords wanted that land. It was improved; it grew crops; it had value. Besides, the crofters tried to expand their holdings up the hills, where the deer and the grouse flourished. So out with them! Let them follow their ancestors to the stews of the cities, or to the empty acres of the Empire.

But the crofters were having none of it, and fought back against all the might of the State assembled against them by the powerful landowners. Gunboats and companies of marines did not intimidate them, and the women especially were not frightened by the police and the special constables. There were pitched battles, and the Government began to fear 'another Ireland'.

The Highland Land Law Association was formed, and it amalgamated with the Sutherland Crofters' Association. It became known as the Land League, and it began to organise the election of MPS. Under the new Reform Acts, the electoral roll had risen by over 8,000 new voters, and many crofters were now entitled to vote.

Up to then, the MPS had automatically been landlords or their representatives – the member for Sutherland was the Duke's eldest son. He had been in the House for ten years, but had never spoken. In the General Election of 1884, crofters' candidates stood against the sitting members, but lost. However, by 1886 there were six crofter MPS, and the Crofters' Bill, as it was known, became law. It gave security of tenure to the crofter, and protected him from the rapacity of landlords. It incidentally introduced other strains into Highland society, but on the whole it had to be seen as a great progressive measure.

The inconspicuous plaque on the bridge at Gartymore commemorates a struggle long and bitter, and sometimes violent, and one which is hardly known today.

The old castle of Helmsdale has gone, demolished in 1970 to make way for the new road bridge. There was not much of it left by then, but in its day it had been a favourite hunting lodge of the Sutherlands. The complicated chain of events which culminated in the burning of Dornoch began in Helmsdale castle, when a guest, Isobel Sinclair, attempted to poison the son of the Earl of Sutherland so that her own son might inherit the title and lands. Unfortunately, it was her own son who drank the poisoned wine and died, as did the Earl and his wife. Isobel Sinclair was arrested and sentenced to death, but died, perhaps by suicide, the night before her execution. The Earl's son was taken into the guardianship of the Earl of Caithness, who, it has long been suspected, had himself instigated the plot.

Later the Murrays intervened in the already tangled picture, and the culmination was that the Sinclairs and the McKays burned Dornoch, as has already been described.

At Helmsdale, of course, you have the choice of going up the Strath of Kildonan, and straight on for the north coast, or of continuing up the east coast to the extreme tip of the mainland. We shall go that way, and return later to the strath.

Just north-east of Helmsdale you go across the Ord, a narrow pass where the road has risen steeply from the plains of Sutherland.

A little further on, and the road drops down to Ousdale. From there you can see a track green now, and overgrown, winding off over the cliff top. This was the old Ord road, notorious and feared amongst travellers for its steepness and bad weather. It was a military road, of course, and the military were not meant to be inconvenienced by steepness or proximity to vertical cliffs falling hundreds of feet to thundering seas. If you walk that track you come to Badbea. Alternatively you can park just off the A9 at the indicated place, and stroll over to the village.

Badbea was built by tenants evicted from Ousdale, just a little further north. It is deserted now, but you can well see the hardship those people must have suffered. The only place to build their hovels was so close to the cliff edge that both children and animals had to be tethered with ropes lest they go over the edge. They stayed there only a couple of generations, and then migrated to New Zealand, and flourished. In the early

years of this century, a descendant came back to Badbea and erected the tablet there, bearing the names of those who emigrated.

The estate from which those families came was owned by Sir John Sinclair, the best known, and in some ways the best, of the agricultural 'improvers' of the early nineteenth century. From his writings, he appears to have been a man of great foresight and compassion; from his actions it is clear that he was just as ruthless, greedy and inhumane as his landowning neighbours. He had written that amongst the duties of a landlord was the obligation to treat tenants fairly, and that a proprietor was no more than a trustee for the public. When he needed the Ousdale lands for his flock of Cheviot sheep, the people were moved out, to the clifftops of Badbea, and left to live or die as best they could.

Sinclair had been a pupil of Adam Smith, and perhaps those who today claim the mantle of Adam Smith would defend the actions of Sinclair. They should know that the memory of Sir John Sinclair has been execrated from Vancouver to Dunedin, wherever the people of Caithness have met together after the great diaspora.

It was the Cheviot sheep of Sir John Sinclair that showed how much money could be taken from the hills and fells. His first flock of 500 ewes was derided by his neighbours, but when they rapidly increased to 2,000, and did themselves well, others copied him, and the clearances began in earnest.

Of course the Cheviots did well, for a while. They had the fertility of generations to support them. Those hills and moors had sent many thousands of cattle to the south every year for many years, and the cattle had kept the land well fertilised and cropped. Sheep benefited for a year or two, and then the accumulated richness failed to meet all the demands made upon it, and the sheep did not do so well, and they did not crop the land the way the cattle did, so that weeds and rank growth spread. Soon, there was more money to be made by renting the land to rich 'sportsmen' who got their sick thrills by slaughtering wild life. So the sheep, in their turn, began to disappear.

There are fine views of the Caithness mountains just north of Ousdale. They are not particularly high, but are shapely. Morven is the highest, at 2,318 feet, and to the east Scaraben has no less than three summits, the highest at 2,054 feet. There are lovely Gaelic names to many of the smaller hills: Smean, Carn Mhor, Salvaich, while, not Gaelic, the shapely Maiden Pap shows modestly to the north.

The broch at Ousdale is reasonably well preserved, and well worth the walk down to the mouth of the burn.

Berriedale has a dramatic position, with the road swooping down from the cliffs into the sheltered and wooded strath. There is a new bridge across the river now, and traffic need hardly pause in its rush north or south. I suggest that you will find a stop here very worthwhile.

The Longwell Water and the Berriedale Water join here, and the merged rivers force their way to the sea through a gorge and past a crag. On that crag you have to look closely to see them – there are a few courses of masonry, all that remains of the old Berriedale Castle, and up on the braes by Langwell House are the few scattered remnants of another castle, that of Achastle. Little is known of either of them; they may well have been those most enviable of places, Highland Castles without a history.

But those castles are no more than brash young upstarts compared to the ancient settlements up the valleys of the two rivers. There is a great wealth of brochs, souterains (underground storage chambers) and cairns running all along the valleys and as far as the slopes of Morven. Walks up either river (the Langwell has a good track for several miles) are lovely, and always interesting, especially if you keep your eyes open for those very ancient monuments.

Several miles up the valley of the Berriedale Water a plaque marks the place where the Duke of Kent was killed on the night of 25th August 1942. The plane he was piloting, a Sunderland Flying Boat, flew into the hillside in thick fog.

The Ord and Berriedale mark a very clear distinction between what has gone before and the lonely, lovely desolation of Caithness. This is a bare country, a country elemental under big skies.

Neil Gunn lived in this country and wrote of it. He thought Sutherland is alluring and feminine, while Caithness is elemental and masculine, and one can see what he means. Certainly they are different, and the difference comes about quite abruptly. Beyond doubt, they both have their beauties and attractions, some blatant and some subtle and needing to be searched for. And equally beyond doubt, both can cast a spell on the visitor. If Gunn was right, and there is a masculine and a feminine here, and if I am right that both can seduce, what are the conclusions?

The road for Dunbeath runs magnificently north, along cliffs, and then dips down into the town. For the best view of the castle at Dunbeath, go down to the harbour, and walk along the track. You can glimpse the castle from the main road, but that is hardly enough. The castle is white and stands prominently on a cliff. What we see today is not all that old – only seventeenth century – but there has been a castle here since the fourteenth century.

It has had its moments of history. In 1650 it was besieged and captured by Montrose. The Marquis of Montrose arrived in Orkney to try to raise Scotland in support of Charles II. He reached the mainland with 1,700 men, mostly German and Danish mercenaries, and raised the Stuart standard at Thurso. He called, and nobody came. Well, just a few did, but the Earl of Caithness and Lord Reay did not, and without them there was no real hope.

Montrose marched his men off south and invested Dunbeath, but only briefly for the Sinclair garrison surrendered because their water supply ran out. Montrose left a small detachment at Dunbeath, and marched off to defeat at Carbisdale, and execution in Edinburgh. Somehow the life and death of Montrose, and what happened after his death, seem like some great Greek tragedy, which moved along inevitably, killing off the best and brightest, testing the bravery and exposing the perfidy of humanity.

In his previous campaign, the Year of Montrose, 1644-5, he had galloped over Scotland from victory to victory. He united the clans and he showed genius in defeating the enemies of his king. The Civil War in Britain produced many remarkable military leaders, not least Cromwell himself. None was more remarkable than Montrose, and none more victorious, until that day in the wild Sutherland hills when he was cornered near the head of the Dornoch Firth and his little army of mercenaries and a few fishermen from Orkney was hacked to pieces by a much superior Covenanting force.

Montrose fled, and finally came to the doors of McLeod of Assynt. He was the Judas who betrayed Montrose for gold, and whose name is still, justly, bracketed with that of the traitor Sir John Menteith, who sold Wallace.

Montrose was taken to Edinburgh, and hanged there, and even the hangman was in tears as he adjusted the noose, and the crowd at the Mercat Cross refused to stone him, although they had been gathered and paid to do so.

So Montrose was hanged, and then his body was cut down and hacked into pieces. His head went on a spike over the Canongate, and his limbs were sent off to the cities of Scotland as a warning. The trunk was buried at the Boroughmuir, but two days later friends dug it up, and took out the heart.

This might seem strange to us, but to them it was following a great tradition, for the heart of Robert the Bruce had been taken out, and was carried on a crusade towards Jerusalem. It was lost in battle. And Devorgila, who founded Sweetheart Abbey in distant Galloway, had carried the embalmed heart of her dead young husband for many years. There was nothing outrageous in seeking to follow such examples.

Besides, the son of Montrose, the young Marquis, was in exile on the Continent, in the company of Lord Napier, one of Montrose's most ardent supporters. It was the wife of Lord

Napier who ordered and arranged the removal of the heart, and had it embalmed and put into a steel box made from the blade of Montrose's sword. The steel box was itself enclosed in a box of gold filigree, and sent off to the young Marquis in Holland. This was one memento of his gallant father that he would not easily forget.

And then it disappeared. Perhaps the young Marquis did not take sufficient care of it. Perhaps he was so busy with his own passionate involvement in Scottish politics and violence that somehow he forgot about the relic. Or perhaps he felt that the whole thing was rather ghoulish. Anyway, for whatever reason, it disappeared for many years, until one day the great-grandson of Lady Napier happened to be in Holland, and mentioned the story in passing to a Dutch friend. The Dutchman knew the box, although he did not know what it contained. It was in the possession of a collector, who was also ignorant of its contents. The collector gladly let it return to the Napier family.

Many years later, the box and its precious contents were in the possession of Lord Napier's daughter. She married Samuel Johnson, who received an appointment in Madras. On their voyage there, their ship was attacked by a French vessel, and in the battle the delicate gold filigree box was totally shattered, but the steel box was undamaged.

One of the first things Mrs. Johnson did when she arrived in Madras was to have a goldsmith rebuild the gold box, and also make a fine silver urn engraved with the story of the exploits of Montrose, and the history of his heart.

One day the urn, filigree box, steel box and heart all disappeared. They had been stolen, and no efforts, no offered reward, brought them back again, although there were rumours that a certain rajah had bought it, in the belief that it must be very powerful, and would ensure that he who owned it would never be a prisoner, nor die in battle.

Twenty more years passed, and a son born to the Johnsons was out hunting one day with some princely Indians, and acquitted himself so well that the rajah who was suspected of having the urn asked the young man how he could show his respect and regard. So young Johnson asked outright for the urn and its contents, and it was given to him.

But even that was not the end of it. The Johnsons were returning home in 1792, and were travelling through France. They were in Boulogne, and about to board a ship for England when the revolutionary French Government ordered that no gold or silver could be exported. Mrs. Johnson entrusted the heart and its boxes and their urn to a friend who was living in France.

It was 1815 before the end of the wars meant that Mrs. Johnson could get back to France and recover her sacred relic. It was not to be. That good friend, Mrs. Knowles, was dead, and no-one knew what had happened to her possessions. Finally, the heart of Montrose was lost, and this time it has remained lost.

Or has it? There have been reports recently that in fact the heart came to light again in 1931, in Canada. It has passed, it is said, between various owners, and now, confusingly, there are two separate claimants each of whom claims to hold the true and only heart of Montrose.

We were in Dunbeath, and looking at Dunbeath Castle before getting side-tracked by the romance of Montrose. The present owner of the castle is an American, and he lives there. He has produced a rather remarkable Manifesto, which is worth reproducing:

The Dunbeath Strath has been prized and used for the support of human life for thousands of years. This unique geological and historical place should be continued through time as a unified whole. To that end, I intend to initiate and support efforts to explore, study, preserve and maintain the prehistoric and historic sites and structures of Dunbeath in harmony with the ongoing contemporary life of Dunbeath Village, the crofts, the grazings and the deer forest. None should be sacrificed for the good of the others. All should accommodate and support the whole.

My goal will be to preserve and maintain each of the above, so that all can survive and live together.

R. Stanton Avery
Dunbeath Castle,
September 1983.

R. Stanton Avery is the moving spirit of the Dunbeath Preservation Trust. This and the sentiments expressed in his Manifesto, are new in Scotland, and wholly admirable. Here is a major Highland landowner (Dunbeath Estate extends to 33,000 acres) actually seeking to do something other than extract the last penny of profit from the land and the people.

To the visitor, the most obvious sign of what is happening at Dunbeath is the Heritage Centre run by the Dunbeath Preservation Trust. This is in the former village school, and is a grand display, showing Dunbeath from its earliest beginnings to the present day. There is a quiet recording of birdsong, and some lovely stained glass embellished by quotations from the writings of Neill Gunn, Dunbeath's most famous son, who actually began his education in that very room.

Do take time for the audio-visual. It is superbly well done, and quite beautiful. If you are particularly interested in the history of the area, or of the people who have lived there, do enquire of the ladies who operate the Centre. Their patience and kindness are boundless, and they know their way around the archives which the Trust is building so assiduously. The very large binoculars on a stand facing out to sea will enable you to look at the oil rigs of the Beatrice Field, only twelve miles off shore, and the only field visible from the mainland.

There are some delightful walks around Dunbeath, and if you know the novels of Neill Gunn, you will recognise much of what he wrote about. He was born in 1891, and although he left for the south to work as a civil servant, he returned to the north as soon as his writing career allowed him to do so. If you walk up the Strath Trail, you will be walking up Gunn's Highland River.

The broch at Dunbeath is well preserved and down at the harbour there is a very fine example of an ice house dug into the hillside.

Just a mile north of Dunbeath is the Laidhay Croft Museum, right on the A9. As the name implies, this is a museum of crofting, and the buildings housing the exhibition are as interesting as the exhibits themselves. The main building is a long-house, in which living quarters, stable and byre were all connected together under the same roof. This very efficient design of farmhouse was normal until quite late in the nineteenth century. The walls are local whinstone rubble bonded with mud mortar, but the roof timbers have had to be replaced, and are a bit incongruous, although the thatching is genuine enough. There is a fine jumble of exhibits, not all of them connected with crofting, but just with life as lived a few years ago. It is the sort of delightful mixed-up place where you will certainly see things that strike a chord with you. 'I remember those!' or even 'We still use these!'

The barn, off to the back of the house, is interesting mainly because of its roof construction. They are the original timbers, and are any old bits of wood that could be found, perhaps washed up on the shore, or rescued from some other use. There are a couple of old oars there, and what is perhaps a bit of mast, and the main crucks holding the roof are cunningly crafted from bits of gnarled tree trunk almost certainly washed up on the shore.

The obvious scarcity of timber here in this treeless countryside indicates just how vicious was the burning of houses during the Clearances. The most valuable thing those peasants owned were their roof timbers. Burn them, and you made it impossible for them to build a new dwelling. No new dwelling, and they had to go elsewhere.

The land was not always treeless. Once it was forested from end to end. It was, needless to say, the depredations of man which removed the woodlands, but that was long ago. Obviously, the first peoples to live here used timber for their dwellings, and that is why there is no clear trace of those dwellings today. They used the plentiful stones for their cairns and tombs, and there are plenty of those around, and soon we shall be visiting some of them.

When the glaciers retreated from this land, about 10,000 years ago, they left the rocks planed down to the very bones. And that was not surprising, for the glaciers were 2,000 feet thick. As the ice retreated, the plants advanced, and by the time the first humans appeared, about 4,500 years ago, the land was well forested. Those people lived together in small villages, tilling some soil and growing barley. They hunted a little and built fishtraps in the sea. We have no idea whether those earliest peoples were the ancestors of the Picts, or whether the Picts were some totally different people who moved in from elsewhere. In fact, we know very little at all about the Picts, except that they had a most remarkable skill in incising stone.

The first we hear of them in history was in 297 AD when the Roman historian Eumenius wrote of Caldones aliique Picti – 'The Caledonians otherwise the Picts', and to the Romans that was the collective name for all people living north of the Forth and Clyde. To the people of southern Britain they were the Priteni, and to the Irish, the Cruithni. We have no idea what they called themselves. In fact, of all the peoples who have lived in Scotland, only the Picts are silent.

They were threatened on all sides. The Scots from Ireland (and, surprisingly, the Scots originated in Ireland) were encroaching from the south-west, and the Britons from the south-east. In 794 AD the Norsemen came, and the last Pictish king was killed fighting them in 839. By 850, Picts and Scots were united under Kenneth MacAlpin, and the Picts as a separate people passed out of history. Perhaps one day someone, somewhere, will find the key to decipher their Ogam script, and we shall learn more about them.

For centuries, of course, Caithness was hardly part of Scotland. The Norsemen laid claim to it, and even after 1472 when the area was formally part of the Scottish kingdom, it was so remote and so wild that the writ of the Crown hardly ran there. From Helmsdale north, the country was a battle-field with the Sutherlands striving against the Earls of Caithness, when the law was the whim of the strongest man, and right was determined by the sword.

It would be pointless and tedious, as well as nauseating, to detail the struggles and mayhem of those centuries. Let it suffice to note that today the native peoples of Caithness and Sutherland are different from those in the rest of Scotland. Their language is different, and their culture is different.

You can't be surprised at this, for until the eighteenth century there were no roads in the area, and to both the Kingdom of Scotland and later to London, this far north-land was just a distant and troublesome appendage. It was only in 1803 that roads began to penetrate these lands. There had been some military roads before that, but few of them, and opening up of the country only came with the 'Parliamentary Roads'.

The Parliamentary Commission for Highland Roads and Bridges got half its finance from the Government, and half from local sources, and with Thomas Telford as engineer, began a programme of building roads, bridges, harbours, piers and even 'Parliamentary' churches and manses. Between 1803 and 1828, nine hundred miles of road were laid, and one thousand one hundred and seventeen bridges built. They are the roads we still travel today, and the A9, north of Dunbeath, is one of them.

Latheron, Lybster, Camster Cairns and Wick

AT LATHERONWHEEL, A SIDE road leads down to a very attractive little harbour. There is a foot-track leading from the harbour over Telford's lovely old bridge and away up the strath, and it is a grand walk.

The adjoining village of Latheron stands at the junction of the direct road to Thurso, the A9. This is the Causewaymire, and it is a fine road through the very heart of Caithness, but for the present we shall keep on to Wick and beyond, using the A99.

The Clan Gunn Society museum is at Latheron, housed in an eighteenth century kirk and in the middle of a truly enormous and still-used grave-yard. Interestingly, the bell-tower of the kirk is not attached to the building, but stands on a brae high above. It was put there so that the sound would spread over a greater area, and call the faithful to their devotions.

Both Latheron and Latheronwheel have tantalised etymologists for years, and there is no agreement on the derivation of the names even today. This is not surprising as Caithness names are the strangest mish-mash, with Gaelic, Norse, Scots, English and perhaps even Pictish influences. Even 'Caithness' itself is mixed, with Cait probably being the Pictish name for the area, and the Norse ness for promontory.

Between the thirteenth and the mid-nineteenth century, Gaelic was the language of the people, and as they always did, Gaels gave names to every detail of the land. No rock, no bend in a river and no hillock went un-named, and in the songs and stories listeners were able to pinpoint exactly where the action took place, because they all knew the names. With the loss of the language the names have been lost too, and today it is only the maps which remind us of the Gaelic heritage, but on the maps only the most prominent features, the mountains and lochs, are named and even then only too many of those names corrupted.

There is not much left now of Forse Castle, which stood on a promontory overlooking the sea. This was a very ancient castle indeed, probably Norse, and it is worth visiting to see the design and construction used by those settlers in such distant times.

The next village is Lybster, still an important fishing centre, but not nearly as important as it was in the days when the herring filled every net, and 200 boats worked out of this port alone. Next to Wick and Fraserburgh, it was the third largest herring station, and it prospered. Some of the houses built then are still there, very pleasant and well-designed, and with early nineteenth century dates on their porches.

Due north of Lybster, on the minor road to the left, are the Grey Cairns of Camster. These are one of the great sights and experiences of the north, and should not be missed. On the vast empty moorlands are two vast cairns of grey rock. One is round, with a single chamber, and the other long, with at least two and possibly more chambers. This long cairn has arms extending from one end, almost enclosing an arena-like space, and one is driven to imagine rites and ceremonies being conducted here, although there is not the slightest evidence that such things ever happened.

Somewhere between four and five thousand years ago, the people built these great cairns to hold their dead. Who those people were and who their dead were, we do not know, any more than we can understand how they were organised to move those many thousands of tons of stone and build them up in that way. And it is not a haphazard piling of stone upon stone.

The burial chambers were beautifully constructed, with corbelled dry stone roofs, and every sign of high craftsmanship. How do we know this? Simple! They are still there, and if you are prepared to crouch, or crawl along the narrow twisting passage, you can get into the middle of the cairns and stand up in the beautifully crafted chambers. Human and animal remains were found there, and some pottery and even pieces of stone from the Isle of Arran, on the other side of the country, which indicates trade of some sort, and trade routes, four thousand years ago.

The track over to the cairns from the road is carefully laid out with old sleepers, and it is dry, and it all feels very open and enjoyable, under the big skies of Caithness. See it now, while it is still open to the skies, for the dreaded forestry is approaching fast, with its awful, sterilising blocks of green conifers.

If you wish, you could go on to Wick by continuing on the road past the cairns, and over the moor to Watten, where you would turn right for Wick and the north. If you do that, though, you will miss some things of great interest on the A99 between Lybster and Wick, and so it is suggested you return the way you came, back from Camster towards Lybster and the A99.

Just off the road, about a mile past Lybster, are the mysterious Stone Rows. There is a signpost to the 'Hill o' Many Stanes' at Clyth. This very strange place is probably contemporaneous with the Camster Cairns, but no-one has the least idea of why it was constructed.

It consists of over two hundred flagstone boulders let into the ground in twenty-two parallel rows, running north to south. They only rise a couple of feet above the soil, and fan out slightly at the south. The broad faces are in line with the rows, and it has been calculated that if the pattern of the rows was complete, over six hundred stones would have been used. Perhaps, even more probably, they were complete, and many of those very useful stones have been lifted and used elsewhere in the past couple of thousand years.

You can speculate and dream about those strange stone rows as you wish, and read into them what you will. Your most outlandish speculation is just as likely to be correct as the latest learned paper from a distinguished archaeologist.

Whaligoe, about 3 miles up the main road from the Hill o' Many Stanes, is a place that really should not be missed. It is unique. I suppose you have to call it a harbour, and certainly fishing boats used it during the herring boom. But the only landward approach to it is down a flight of over three hundred steps from the cliff top to a tiny platform above the water. Local people will tell you there are 365 steps, one for each day of the year, but I counted 352 on my way down, and lost count at 290 on my way up.

The seaward entrance to the jetty is hardly less difficult than the landward. The boats had to be pulled in stern-first, for there is no room to turn in the cove. Nevertheless, in 1828, twenty-four boats worked out of the harbour.

The flagstone steps, with occasional resting places, cost £8 to build, and building the platform and clearing out the cove another £53. There was no space down on the jetty for gear, so nets as well as fish had to be carried up those steps every day. Of course, that was women's work.

If you suffer at all from vertigo, do not attempt the climb down to the platform, which Thomas Telford called 'a dreadful place.' In truth, there is nothing much to see or do when you get there, except contemplate the climb back up. Still, if you do it, the sense of achievement is considerable. Don't try to do what the women did every day 150 years ago – climb up and down half a dozen times in quick succession, each time carrying up to a hundredweight of net or a cran of herring.

North, again, then, to Wick the place which Robert Louis

Stevenson called The meanest of man's towns, situated certainly on the baldest of God's bays. He exaggerated.

There is an airport at Wick and it used to be an R.A.F. station. To all airmen, that was the equivalent of Siberia. If you were posted to Wick you were in trouble, you had been in trouble, or you were going to be in trouble. It is not exactly a prepossessing town, although perhaps my view is jaundiced by memory. Anyone whose chief recollection of a place is of refuelling a Coastal Command Hudson in the pre-dawn darkness of a January day in Wick is entitled to be prejudiced.

Prepossessing or not, though, Wick is interesting. The name came from the Norse Vik meaning 'bay', and Wick Bay is one of the very few natural harbours on this stern and rock-bound coast. It would be natural for the longships from Norway to make for haven here, and the Orkney Saga says that Wick was the place where the Earls of Orkney sometimes stayed.

They would have stayed in Old Wick Castle, to the south of the town. This is one of the oldest castles in Scotland – perhaps only Castle Sween in distant Argyll is older.

Dating from the twelfth century, and of course much ruined, it still stands perhaps forty feet high on the rocky promontory between two ravines running down to the sea. There is a deep ditch on the landward side. There is no door or gate to the castle, and presumably entry was by some wooden stairway arrangement to an upper storey, some arrangement that could be demolished or pulled up if the castle was attacked.

There is not a lot to be seen now of this ancient place, but I have found few more contented moments in life than sitting on the grass here, back to the wall of the castle, pipe drawing well, and looking out over the silvery sea. Personal happiness or enjoyment is a poor reason to recommend anything to anyone, but try it: perhaps the quietness and sense of great history will affect you too.

Something else that makes it imperative to visit Wick is the Heritage Centre. This is another of those modern Interpretation Centres which can help to bring a vivid understanding to places and their history.

The centre is in Bank Row, near the harbour built by Thomas Telford (who else?) in 1810. There are fishermen's cottages, and outbuildings and a kippering shed and the cooperage. There is also a full-scale harbour with three boats and a completely restored fisherman's house from ninety years ago. This is the only museum in the country with a restored and fully functioning lighthouse. Altogether, you can learn as much, or even more, than you want to learn about the old herring industry in the exhibition, and a couple of hours spent there will be hours well spent.

Allow more than a couple of hours, though, if you get immersed in the amazing archive of Caithness photographs. They were taken by the Johnston family of Wick and are a record of Caithness in all its aspects from 1863 until 1950. If you have Caithness connections of any kind, you are likely to find a photographic link here, and the archivists are only too willing to help you.

One thing is sure about the north of Scotland today – there is no shortage of impressive museums and 'Interpretation Centres'. Even in this short run from Dunbeath to Wick we have visited four of them, and each is superb of its kind. There are many others all over Scotland. By going through them all, a visitor would, in a couple of days, have learned more about Scotland than the man in the Morningside bus will ever know. And it is not, these days, all tartan toshery and haggis bashing.

The thought occurs that if any enterprising body collected all such Interpretation Centres together in one place, it would not be necessary for tourists to spend so much time travelling. They could just go to, let us say, the Peter de Savary Centre For Scottish Appreciation (and it need not even be in Scotland) and

visit all the exhibits, and thus Taste Scotland, cheaply and eff-
ciently.

Don't laugh at the idea. It has already been done. Not in
Scotland, true, but in Jakarta there is a huge exhibition called
Indonesia in Miniature, and there, in one day, the visitor can
travel from the north of Sumatra three thousand miles to the
south of New Guinea, and see (perhaps enjoy) a condensed,
sanitized, expurgated and officially approved version of that
vast complex country. If it can be done there, certainly it could
be done here and there would be no need for visitors to be
exposed to the traditional vagaries of Scottish weather and
Scottish cooking. They need not ever again face that most awful
of Highland experiences, the kilted Englishman managing a
Highland Hotel.

But back to Wick the reality, not the nightmare.

The other big attraction in Wick is the Caithness Glass factory,
which welcomes visitors. Glass blowing is a strange occupation,
and whether it is an art or a craft or just plain old boring hard work
I really don't know. Watch it for as long as you like there in Wick
and judge for yourself.

North, then, again, for the last time, to John O' Groats.
Before getting on to the road, though, perhaps you should visit
the strange twin castles of Sinclair and Girnigoe. They are out
at Moss Head, north of Wick just by the lighthouse, and across
the airport runway.

There is not a lot of them left now, but they are fascinating
ruins, even without their fascinating history. Although it is older
than Castle Sinclair, there is more left of Girnigoe. It is mounted on a spit of land running out into the sea between two deep
ravines or geos. To enter it, you actually go through the ruins of
Castle Sinclair. You can see the remains of a spiral staircase and
the great recess of the kitchen fireplace, quite big enough to
hold an ox, and it probably often did. There are steps down to

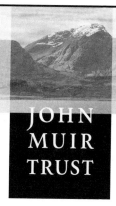

a windowless chamber which might have been a dungeon, and a puzzling passageway leading only to a sheer drop to the sea. Was that perhaps a quick exit route for unwanted guests? A flight of steps leads down through a tunnel to the sea at the tip of the promontory.

It would be tedious to relate the history of the Sinclairs. They are of no more interest than the Sutherlands. Suffice to note that their past is just as blood-boltered and filled with greed and treachery as that of any other Highland family of note and power. They were, of course, the Earls of Caithness, and in constant conflict with their neighbours, the Earls of Sutherland, and the country and people were racked for generations as they struggled.

It was certainly unique, but quite in the family character, when George, the fourth Earl, killed his own son in 1576. The young man was suspected of plotting against his father, and maybe he was, but in any case he was thrust down into the dungeon at Girnigoe, and kept there for six years, until one day his father ordered him to be well fed on salt beef. He then ordered that no water should be given to the young man, who died horribly of thirst. It took a particularly perverted cast of mind to think of killing by thirst in the Highlands.

Just north of Wick on the A99 there is a minor road, the B874 running off left, and eventually to Thurso. It runs by the Wick river and up Loch Watten, and is a pleasant short cut between Wick and Thurso, the two main towns of Caithness. It is not for us today, though, since we are heading for John O' Groats. What is important about this road is that there, between the road and the river, is a Celtic cross, and it marks the site of the last major clan battle in Scotland. That was on 13th July, in 1680, and the battle was between the Campbells and the Sinclairs.

It was, of course, a conflict about money and power. The sixth Earl of Caithness died without a male heir. He had led a life of wild dissoluteness, and to finance his latter years had accepted money from Campbell of Glenorchy in return for his Earldom. Glenorchy, of course, is many miles from Caithness, way off in the south of Argyll, the kingdom of the Campbells. But no Campbell ever missed any opportunity to gain wealth and power. They already had a toe-hold in the east, having acquired Cawdor, near Inverness, by kidnap and forced marriage. Another branch of the Campbells was responsible for that, certainly, but they all had the same driving ambition.

So Campbell of Glenorchy came north to claim what he believed to be his right. George Sinclair of Keiss thought he had a better claim, and in any case was not prepared to accept the Campbell claim. Other lairds of Caithness supported him, and a force was assembled to meet the seven hundred men Glenorchy led north. When the two armies first met, on 12th July, on the south side of the river, it was too late in the day to fight, so the two sides settled down for the night. The Sinclair men went off to Wick.

Legend insists that Glenorchy arranged for a ship with a cargo of whisky to be wrecked on the Wick shore that night, while another legend has it that he arranged for smugglers to broach the casks in their cellars. Anyway, it seems certain that the Sinclairs spent the night in a whisky-sodden carousel, and when they took the field in the morning were in no condition to either run or fight. Those lucky enough to be mounted escaped, but about two hundred men of Caithness died on the field.

So Glenorchy became Earl of Caithness for six troubled years, during which time his tenants were in constant revolt against him. George Sinclair actually besieged and took Sinclair castle, the Earl's seat, although he was not there at the time. Eventually, Glenorchy gave up the Earldom to George Sinclair, and accepted other titles and lands instead.

On the road again, the tall tower you can see to the right, in

Sinclair's Bay, is the Ackergill Tower. It is about seventy feet high, and was built in the fifteenth century, although much modernised and changed in the 1850s. For a closer look you have to walk along the beach from Ackergill, but the tower is privately owned and occupied, and it would be impolite to wander around it.

Keiss, and Keiss Castles, stand at the north of Sinclair's Bay. There are two castles, one standing square on the cliffs and continuing to defy the elements as it has done for more than 300 years. The other is much younger, no older than mid-eighteenth century, and is still occupied, although not now by a Sinclair.

A minor road to the left, just before Keiss, leads off to Lyth and its Arts Centre. It is more than a little surprising to find an Arts Centre in such an isolated place, and perhaps especially one so fine and successful as this. There is a studio-theatre, and when you visit you can't be sure whether you will see an exhibition of contemporary art or a performance by some touring company. I suppose one should never be surprised at what happens in the Highlands these days, but an Arts Centre at Lyth, for example, and a very good bookshop at Inverkirkaig, continue to surprise and delight me, at least.

Beyond Keiss the road, on its last stretch towards John O' Groats, goes past Nybster, sometimes called 'The Dog's Nose' because it is always cold and wet, and on past Freswick Bay. There was a considerable Norse settlement here, and it is still being excavated at the head of the bay. A Viking longhouse was found (the only one on the Scottish mainland), a bath-house and the usual middens and houses.

Up, then, to Worth Hill and splendid views, at last, of the Orkneys, of the Pentland Firth, and of John O' Groats.

John O' Groats and Thurso

IT WAS A CHINESE SAGE, surely, who wrote that it is better to travel hopefully than to arrive.

He could well have been writing about John O' Groats, for it cannot fail to be an anti-climax. Yes, somehow it is an achievement to arrive there, even if one arrives in some thundering great bus accompanied by a dozen more of its kind. It isn't even that John O' Groats is the northernmost point of the mainland – that distinction belongs to Dunnet Head, some miles away. Perhaps it is the sense that no two places on the mainland are further apart than Lands End and John O' Groats. That has been a challenge for a long time, and people have travelled between the two places in all conceivable ways, walking, running, riding, roller-skating, pushing wheel barrows. It is like swimming the English Channel – somehow, it is the ultimate challenge. But having arrived at John O' Groats, one will possibly wonder just how quickly one can get away.

Stay long enough to absorb the tale of Jan de Groot and his ferry and his quarrelsome family and his octagonal house with its eight doors and its octagonal table.

There are good things around John O' Groats. Go up to Duncansby Head by the lighthouse, and look over the Pentland Firth to the Orkneys. Or you could spend a day on the Orkneys, not that you will absorb much from those wonderful islands in one day. Or you can go wandering along the beaches, no doubt picking up shells and admiring them, for many of them on these beaches come from deep water species, and are unfamiliar to us.

Think about the Pentland Firth, too, calm or stormy. This is one of the fiercest stretches of water in the world, and has been the death of many a ship and many a sailor. The Admiralty Pilot warns that ships entering the Firth should be prepared to batten down even in the finest weather, as the transition from smooth water to broken seas is so sudden. Yet this is the way to Scandinavia and the Baltic, and the route all ships from the east coast had to take on their way to the Americas. Coracles, long-ships, schooners, trawlers, sloops, yawls, steamers and now oil tankers have all plied their trade in these waters, and all too often have perished.

The Pentland Firth is the narrow funnel between the Atlantic ocean and the North Sea, and for fourteen hours every day the sea pours through from the Atlantic and for ten hours every day it floods back again. Some parts are ebbing while others are still flooding, there is a rocky seabed and high winds and the result is a confusion of seas.

There is the Swelkie, just north of Stroma island – that is the island nearest the mainland. The Swelkie is a whirlpool. The Norsemen knew it, and feared it, and named it Svelgr. Under certain conditions, and they are not infrequent, there is a whirling pit in the sea, and it is death to boats and sailors.

And this is not just your ordinary, common-or-garden death-to-all-sailors whirlpool. This one is caused by the magic mill pouring out all the salt in the sea. The mill belonged to King Frodi, and it would produce anything it was ordered to produce – salt, flour, gold, anything at all. The Sea King Mysing stole the mill and sailed away with it. Just off Stroma, Mysing sat down to his dinner and found it needed salt. So he ordered the magic mill to produce salt for him. It immediately did so, but then, too late, Mysing recalled that he had not learned how to stop the mill working. So it worked away, producing salt, and Mysing's boat was filled with salt and sank and the mill sank and it is still there, churning out salt, and its frantic rotation often causes that fearful whirlpool.

There are no legends about the Bores of Duncansby, and the Merry Men o' Mey. Perhaps they are too frightening to have legends. You can see the Bores from John O' Groats – the breakers off-shore. The Merry Men are a truly frightening sight. They occur off St John's Point, to the west of John O' Groats. Sometimes, when the ebbing tide meets the reef there is a violent tumult of water as far as nine miles off-shore. These are not just breaking waves, but great smashing pillars of water thirty or forty feet high, roaring with a viciousness never forgotten, while the spume of their anger is blown far inland. No boat lives when the Merry Men dance, and no sailor faces them.

The name 'Pentland Firth' comes, like so much else, from the Norse – Pettal ands fiorthr – The Strait of the Land of the Picts. It is only seven miles across, but the tide-rip can exceed ten knots, and that is enough to drive many a sailing ship backwards, and trouble many a steamer of an earlier age. It used to be that ships took on a pilot to see them safely through the Firth, and more than one pilot found himself carried off to Canada or New York when the captain refused to shorten sail and let him off.

If you walk over to Duncansby you can add a few thrills to your holiday. Go to the Long Geo south of the lighthouse and peer over the cliff. It is really quite safe, and there is a rail at the edge, but you are looking down two hundred vertical feet, and there is an overhang, so there is nothing but very thin air between you and the water so far below.

West of the lighthouse is the Glupe, and you have to be really careful there. There is a tunnel in the cliffs at sea level, and an opening from that tunnel at the top of the cliffs. In stormy weather, when the waves thunder in to the tunnel, spray rises likes steam from the Glupe. You can cross the natural bridge and peer down into the depths. There is nothing to see, and all is darkness and gloom, but at least you will have done something that no purchasers of postcards at John O' Groats will have done.

South of the lighthouse the cliffs diminish, and you can get down to a shingle beach and walk along to the Duncansby Stacks, three pillars of rock detached from the cliff face, and the home of myriad sea birds. To get to them, you must go through the Thirl Door, which is a natural hole in the rocks, and is in fact another stack in the earliest geological days of its making. The Stacks are the Muckle, the Peedie and the Tom Thumb, and they are a fantastic sight close up.

As an alternative to walking and climbing along the beach to visit them, you can take a boat trip from John O' Groats, and the boatmen usually have a wealth of information about the birds you will see in such numbers.

These are fish-rich waters still, or comparatively so, and the seabirds swarm. Gannets, skuas, gulls, fulmars, guillemots, cormorants, puffins – they are all here, so please do take great care not to disturb them in their nesting season.

Travelling further now, we must take the A836 to the west, to Thurso and beyond.

It is bare and treeless country, but not by any means barren. You will notice that most houses and farms have their peat stacks, and the moor is sprinkled with the hags where the peats are cut. The peat comes free, of course, except for the very considerable labour of cutting, stacking, and carrying it.

You will also notice the many fences here made from slabs of Caithness flagstone let into the ground. They make a very strong and a very long-lasting fence. Hedges would be difficult to grow in this windy and surf-blasted land, but a good flagstone fence will give excellent shelter to sheep and lambs. Those flagstones are a fine, hard, sedimentary rock which splits easily and wears well, and in the days when long life and good value were a consideration, they were used to pave half the world. There are none worked today.

The Castle of Mey lies behind the woods to the right of the road, and looks out over the waters of the Firth. This little castle was bought by the Queen Mother in 1952, and she still spends a good deal of time there, obviously relishing the austere beauty of Caithness. It is quite an old castle, sixteenth century probably, but of course has been modernised more than once. It is private property, and not open to the public, although the gardens sometimes are.

You don't have to follow the main road hereabouts, and indeed unless you are in a hurry it is better not to. Go off on the minor coast roads and wander along. You won't get lost, really, and it would not matter if you did, because keeping the sea on your right will inevitably bring you back to the A836. Scarfskerry, Harrow, Ham and others are small villages on these coast roads, and there are some attractive harbours, from which, once, the Caithness flagstones were exported, after being cut and polished at the factories whose ruins we can still see. Usually they were built, understandably, in flagstone, and show what a useful and adaptable material it was.

The ferries used to run from here to Orkney. There were two of them, one for people and the other for animals, especially horses, for there used to be a considerable trade in horses between Orkney and the mainland.

You really should go out to Dunnet Head, if for no better

reason than to boast that you really have stood on the most northerly point of the British mainland, while all the bus parties at John O' Groats only think they have. But in fact there are better reasons than that.

Dunnet Head is a grand, sea-girt moorland, dotted with lochans and surrounded by lovely red cliffs. Dunnet Bay is a great stretch of sand, smooth and delightful, one of Scotland's best beaches, and of course, if you are hardy enough to swim, the water is clear and pure.

There is a cave under the low cliffs, where a visiting mermaid once imprisoned her human lover, and there is also a rock at the north of the bay, clearly marked by the imprint of the Devil's foot; knee and fingers. He had jumped across the bay from Castletown, and stumbled as he landed, and the rocks were left indelibly marked.

The lighthouse is magnificent. The lantern is 346 feet above sea level, and it was built in 1831. Of course, it faces some of the roughest seas and roughest weather in the world, difficult as that may be to believe on some golden day when the whole world gleams in jewelled colours. And such days are not uncommon. But also not uncommon are days when the winds shriek and the spray flies over the cliff tops and the ground shakes to the thundering impact of breakers. The lighthouse has seen it all, many times over, but the visitor has not, and be it a golden or thundering day, a visit to Dunnet Head will long be remembered.

Going back to the main road from the Head, you skirt St John's Loch. If you are unwell, stop there and try its healing powers. For hundreds of years it was believed to work and perhaps it did, and perhaps it still will work if only you believe in it. Your illness must be chronic, of body or mind – no use seeking help for a broken leg. You must go to the loch on the first Monday of a summer month, and arrive there at gloaming. Bathe in the loch, give it an offering of money, walk round it clockwise and be gone before sunrise. Fail to do any of these, and the influence will not be benign.

Today, the loch is better known for the size and fighting qualities of its trout than for healing leprosy or those stricken with the palsy.

Castletown, at the south side of Dunnet Bay, was once the centre of the flagstone industry, thanks to the initiative of John Traill – and the hard work of the quarrymen. Traill was the local landlord, having been canny enough to marry the daughter of the Earl of Caithness. That was a good stroke for the son of the local minister. He was guilty of clearing some crofters off his lands, but on the other hand he did provide employment in growing flax and weaving linen, and also, on a much bigger scale, manufacturing and exporting flagstones. By the end of the nineteenth century, about five hundred men were employed there, and Castletown harbour was a busy place indeed.

The road runs straight for Thurso. Just beyond the village of Markle, at the top of the small hill, there is a little castelated building, Harald's Tower. It is not particularly old, and was built by Sir John Sinclair as a burial vault. It stands on the site of a much older building, a chapel put up to mark the spot where, long ago, a Norseman was killed in some dynastic battle. After his death, a strange glow was seen night after night at the spot where he fell, and so the chapel was built to venerate him. There are some who say that even today a sort of strange glow lights up the ground around Harald's Tower.

CHAPTER 9

Thurso, Melvich, Dounreay and Bettyhill

THURSO IS THE MAJOR TOWN of the north coast, and a major road centre, with roads radiating in all directions but north, and that is sea. It is a pleasant town, neat and clean, and much larger than it used to be a few years ago, for Thurso is the dormitory for Dounreay, the nuclear plant just a few miles down the road. The incomers, collectively known as 'The Atomics', have transformed the town, and in some ways improved it.

This is the town of Sir John Sinclair, one of those remarkable men whose energies seemed inexhaustible, whose curiosity was insatiable and whose abilities were boundless. He was also pigheaded, sometimes unfeeling and often unscrupulous. There is a statue of him in the centre of town, wearing the trews and plaid of the Fencible Regiment he raised and commanded during the Napoleonic Wars. The Fencibles were the Territorials of their day, but were used to quell civil unrest and

> **TREES FOR LIFE**
>
> is a Scottish charity whose aim is to regenerate and restore the native Caledonian Forest to a large area of the Highlands of Scotland and to recreate a balanced forest ecosystem.
>
> You can support us by becoming a member and/or joining us on a volunteer work week in the Highlands. For more information please contact us at:
>
> Trees for Life, The Park, Findhorn Bay, Forres IV36 3TZ.
> Tel. 01309 691292
> web site: www.treesforlife.org.uk
>
> **Join us and help the return of the Caledonian Forest!**
>
>
>
> TREES FOR LIFE

protest. Indeed, they were often seen as being the executive arm of the landowner's power.

Sir John had attended school at Harrow with Lord Byron and Sir Robert Peel, and even at school showed powers of organisation. Later, Byron described him as 'the prodigy of our schooldays', but he left school at sixteen and went to the Continent, where he was promptly arrested as a spy and taken before Napoleon. The boy managed to persuade the great Corsican that he was no spy, and was sent on his way.

It was Sir John who, by his example and teaching, led Scottish agriculture to its Age of Improvement. He encouraged enclosures of common land, he encouraged the Cheviot sheep flocks, he encouraged rotation of crops and the growing of turnips as winter feed. It was the Age of Improvement that saw the many miles of stone walling driven over moors and up steep slopes. It was also the Age of Improvement that saw the land cleared of people so that sheep might bring temporary wealth to the landowners, and also saw the mass of people depending on the potato for their food, and suffering incredible hardship when that crop failed.

It was Sir John who organised and edited The Statistical Account of Scotland in 1790, a remarkable publication that gives us more knowledge about Scotland of that day than is available for any other country in the world. The minister of every parish in Scotland was required to report on conditions in his parish, and the reports were in great depth. Sir John himself wrote the report on Thurso, as a model for all others. From his report, we know that then the population was about one thousand, and that people were sober, regular (!) and attentive to business, although keen dancers, which was their only public entertainment. Thurso had two public schools and a number of private ones; there was a Post Office and a Customs House, two very good inns, a cart factory, a tannery and a bank. However, the streets were unpaved and lined with middens. The weather was good for eight months every year, and the scenery grand and picturesque.

Thurso was an important trading port long before Sir John appeared. Agriculture was always important in Caithness, and oats and barley were shipped from Thurso way back in the thirteenth century. The Customs House records go back to 1707, and even the earliest tell of trading in meal, grain, beef, hides, fish, timber, iron, wine, salt and coal. Today, the harbour is empty but for an occasional pleasure craft and a few fishing boats.

Sir John was born in Thurso East Castle, although not in the one whose ruins we see today. They are the ruins of a splendid new castle built in 1872; it was not long before poverty in the family meant that it was deserted and left to ruin however. It had been built on the site of another small castle, itself only seventeenth century, and it was in that one that Sir John was born, the ninth of eleven children.

It is more than a little ironical that after all the 'improvements' initiated by Sir John, Scotland faced its worst agricultural crisis and tragedy ever. To the displaced crofter and small farmer, the potato was a great blessing. It grew easily, and flourished in sandy and peaty soil fertilised by seaweed. So long as there was a store of potatoes at the beginning of winter, then you would not actually starve. So long as you had a store of potatoes...

In 1845, the potatoes rotted in the ground in Ireland, and the people went hungry. In 1846 the potato blight spread to the Highlands where, as in Ireland, the potato had become the staple diet. And the year had been stormy, with poor fishing. Grain had grown well, but that was a crop for big farms, not for poor crofters with a couple of acres. The people were hungry, and then they were starving and then they were dying of disease and malnutrition.

The big farms had done quite well that year. Grain prices were high, and the crops had been good, so the ships were sailing from Wick and Thurso laden with oats and barley, while the men, hungry, and with wives and children starving, watched them loading.

There were food riots, and in February 1847, grain dealers and warehouses in Thurso were attacked and broken open and the grain distributed to the hungry people of the town and round about. It was agreed that the export of grain would be stopped, and sales made locally, but there were many landowners who considered that wrong. It was interference with The Market, that strange god which is worshipped periodically and appealed to when profits are at war with conscience or morality.

They insisted on continuing to export to the south, which was The Natural Market, although it would seem obvious that the real natural market was the empty bellies of the local people.

It is impossible to exaggerate the horrors and miseries of those years when the potato blight struck – for it was not just one year. Even today reading the contemporary reports is harrowing. There was no Bob Geldorf then to prick the conscience of the wealthy and well-fed. Relief, such as it was, was in the hands of the landlords and their agents. Many of them profited greatly from the famine and the relief funds. If nothing else, they got roads and jetties built at no cost, for the indigent had to work for their daily handful of meal, and what better work could there be than driving a road through the Laird's estate or building a jetty to serve the needs of the Big House?

The unrest increased as the hunger and the death lists grew. In Thurso there were riots and marches and landlords were burned in effigy. Some pilots refused to move cargoes of grain. Mobs armed with guns blocked the harbour, and even mounted two cannon to threaten the ships loading at the quay.

It was too much for the authorities. One hundred special

constables were enrolled, and the 76th Regiment marched north from Wick where they had already faced mobs and enforced the loading of grain ships. This was in 1847, and they had to ensure the loading of grain while the people were quite literally dying of hunger. Boats had been put across the roads as barricades, but the special constables escorting the grain carts dragged them to one side. The crowd pressed forward onto the carts and the specials. The Sheriff appeared and read the Riot Act and the men of the 76th fixed their bayonets and moved forward. The crowd fell back and the carts moved on to the quay, where the ships waited.

There was no John Murdoch or John McLean in Thurso or Wick or anywhere in Caithness to give direction to those protests. It was just a crowd of hungry people, a mob in angry despair. There was no leader, and the rioters have now long been forgotten. That is a pity for the story of those food riots is a valuable counter-weight to all the tales of tartan toshery to which the visitor is subjected.

At Thurso, you have to decide where you are going next. Is it to be due west to Melvich and Bettyhill, or back again to Wick and Helmsdale? If you do that from Thurso, you will travel through the heart of Caithness, and that is well worth doing.

In 1770 that great traveller and writer Pennant described Caithness. It may be called, he wrote, 'an immense morass mixed with some fruitful spots of oats and barley, much coarse grass and here and there some fine.' That is a reasonable description of a lot of the country, but certainly not all. There is some extraordinarily good agriculture in the interior of Caithness. Travel south from Thurso, using a map to navigate the considerable network of minor roads, and you will see a lot of cultivation and a lot of cattle. Especially in the straths of the rivers (the Thurso, for example) there are wide fields kept in good heart for grass and grain. There are lots of cattle, many of them these days the quick-growing imports from the Continent.

If you are going south, either on the A9 towards Dunbeath, or on the more interesting winding minor roads to the west, you will come to Mybster, which again is an important road junction.

South of Mybster and you are in country that fulfils Thomas Pennant's description of 'an immense morass.' It has its own sparse and austere beauty, though, and is not the sort of place you should hurry through to get somewhere else.

The name tells us that Spittal, just north of Mybster, is an old settlement, and at some time there has been a shelter there for travellers. One of the Sinclairs tried to raise troops there for the Jacobite cause in 1746, but only forty-three men answered the call. This was not clan country, of course, and there were no clan chiefs to demand that their men follow the standard. The forty-three were volunteers, well armed and mounted, but most of them went to their deaths as they rode away from Spittal that day.

There is a big flagstone quarry at Spittal, no longer worked, of course, but famous as the source of fossil fish. The Caithness flagstone is a sedimentary rock and under it is the Old Red Sandstone. This is unbelievably old, having been laid down perhaps 350 million years ago under the surface of a great lake, Orcadie, which covered the north of Scotland, and much further, in those days. The lake was rich in fish, which were evolving quickly and in many directions at the time, and some of those fish became fossilised. There are so many of them around Spittal, and seeking them became so popular, that it had to be controlled, and now the quarries are owned by the Nature Conservancy Council.

Wander off, if you can, down the minor roads to the west of Mybster, through Westerdale and on, perhaps to Loch More, and even beyond that. This, the Bog of the Seagull – Blarnam Froile – is bogland of international fame as it is still in its undisturbed state, with undisturbed flora and fauna. Better see it soon, before it is too late, and the dreaded tax-advantageous conifers take over.

Just south of Westerdale is the site of what must once have been one of the most attractive castles in this land of castles. There is little of it left now, and you must look hard to see it, but the site is unforgettable. A rocky pinnacle stands proud in the middle of a gorge cut by the river. There is no warning of the gorge until suddenly you find yourself on the edge of this fifty foot high cliff, with the castle menacing you on its pillar of rock. It is quite a remarkable place, and one day, I have long promised myself, I will find a way up to those ruins and wander around the six foot thick walls.

But now we will return to the north coast, and continue our journey westwards from Thurso, along the A836. Scrabster, at the north-west of Thurso Bay, is the car ferry terminal for the Orkneys, and a busy port. Beyond Scrabster, if you walk to Spear Head, Clett and Holborn Head, you will find grand cliffs and some fine isolated beaches.

Just by Bridge of Foss, on the main road, a minor road goes off to the right, up to the sea, and to Crosskirk. Here are the remains of one of the oldest chapels in the country. It dates back to the twelfth century, and was dedicated to St Mary. There is no roof now, but the windowless walls still stand. This little chapel has both nave and chancel, and is one of the earliest to have that separation. The doorway has strange sloping jambs and a large lintel, and those sloping jambs are found only in Orkney and Shetland, and in Ireland; this is the only known example on the mainland. Plainly, it was a Norse design. Crosskirk is a fine and peaceful place – a summer day spent here, pottering around the chapel and graveyard, walking along the cliffs of Brims Ness, and a day spent generally lazing about here would not be a wasted day.

By now you will see the great silver sphere of the United

Kingdom Atomic Energy Authority Dounreay up ahead. It has been declared a Listed Building, and so cannot be dismantled. There are tours around Dounreay, and they are interesting, not just for the tiny glimpse you are given of the workings, but for the utter certainty expressed by the guides that the plant should be there, will be there, and must be constantly extended. You will be told, with utter conviction, of the total safety of the plant, and of how there will be no conceivable or possible problem with storing radioactive material from all over the world for many years. You will be told how the natural radiation from granite rocks is more intense than anything that comes from Dounreay. And then one notices that everyone is wearing radiation exposure films and that there are notices everywhere of what to do if... and one wonders.

Sandside Bay, just to the west of Dounreay, is a most delightful place where there are the remains of prehistoric animals. Indeed, there are prehistoric remains all round the area. Just to the south, on the minor road from Reay to Shebster, there are some interesting burial cairns, but then, there are reminders of the distant past in many places, some of them marked and obvious, but many more just a strange mound in the heather.

West of Reay, the A836 climbs up to moorland, although the sea and spectacular cliffs are never far away.

Melvich is quite delightful. It lies at the mouth of the Halladale River, at the foot of Strath Halladale. There is a grand, quiet road road running the length of the strath, and then over the watershed down the Strath of Kildonan to Helmsdale. That is one of the roads you really must meander down, for rushing down it is pointless and wasteful. There is so much to appreciate that hurrying would be the equivalent of gulping a good malt whisky – if you do that, then it is too good for you!

Walking, birdwatching, beachcombing, fishing, even swimming and surfing are the ways to pass time at Melvich. And you will be amazed, surely, at how the days do pass, as you watch the tides change and the colours change as clouds sweep across the huge sky. Melvich is one of those places where, if the sun is right, one is constantly amazed at the colours. One realises that the picture postcards are really true to life after all, and that one really should not apologise for the holiday photographs – the colours really are like that.

Beyond Melvich the road to Bettyhill shrinks rather in width, but certainly gains in beauty. These miles are certainly amongst the finest that even the north of Scotland has to offer. The road sweeps up and down very satisfyingly, and runs over moorland plentifully supplied with Highland burns. Again, don't hurry on this road, but take off down the side roads, to Strathy Point and Kirtomy, for example. You will be well rewarded by sea scapes of rare beauty and surely you will find sights that will stay long in your memory.

Try spending some time on the beach at Torrisdale Bay, between Skerray and Bettyhill. You might well agree with those who argue that this is the finest beach in all of Scotland.

Look out for the Devil's Stone at Drumholiston, a couple of miles from Melvich. It is a great boulder by the side of the road, neatly sliced in two as though by some great axe. Well, it wasn't an axe, but the Devil's tail. He had spent some time in Melvich, tempting the people there, offering them untold delights and wealth in exchange for their immortal souls, but he found it devilishly hard going in Melvich, where the people rejected him. So off he went to Thurso, where he believed that he would have more success, and as he went he slapped the boulder with his tail so hard that it split in two. Well, that is the story they will tell you in Melvich, but in Thurso I have heard it said that the Devil was going the other way.....

Soon, only too soon, the road comes to Bettyhill, where we have been before, and where we leave this Empty Land.

We may leave it, and perhaps we shall never come back. But it is certain that we shall never forget what we have seen and what we have felt in travelling these many miles of delight.

Some other books published by **LUATH** PRESS

Tales from the North Coast

Alan Temperley

ISBN 0 946487 18 9 PBK £8.99

 Seals and shipwrecks, witches and fairies, curses and clearances, fact and fantasy – the authentic tales in this collection come straight from the heart of a small Highland community. Children and adults alike responsd to their timeless appeal. These *Tales of the North Coast* were collected in the early 1970s by Alan Temperley and young people at Farr Secondary School in Sutherland. All the stories were gathered from the area between the Kyle of Tongue and Strath Halladale, in scattered communities wonderfully rich in lore that had been passed on by word of mouth down the generations. This wide-ranging selection provides a satisying balance between intriguing tales of the supernatural and more everyday occurrences. The book also includes chilling eye-witness accounts of the notorious Strathnaver Clearances when tenants were given a few hours to pack up and get out of their homes, which were then burned to the ground.

Underlying the continuity through the generations, this new edition has a foreward by Jim Johnston, the head teacher at Farr, and includes the vigorous linocut images produced by the young people under the guidance of their art teacher, Elliot Rudie.

Since the original publication of this book, Alan Temperley has gone on to become a highly regarded writer for children.

The general reader will find this book's spontaneity, its pictures by the children and its fun utterly charming. SCOTTISH REVIEW

An admirable book which should serve as an encouragement to other districts to gather what remains of their heritage of folk-tales. SCOTTISH EDUCATION JOURNAL

LUATH GUIDES TO SCOTLAND

These guides are not your traditional where-to-stay and what-to-eat books. They are companions in the rucksack or car seat, providing the discerning traveller with a blend of fiery opinion and moving description. Here you will find *'that curious pastiche of myths and legend and history that the Scots use to describe their heritage... what battle happened in which glen between which clans; where the Picts sacrificed bulls as recently as the 17th century... A lively counterpoint to the more standard, detached guidebook... Intriguing.'*
THE WASHINGTON POST

These are perfect guides for the discerning visitor or resident to keep close by for reading again and again, written by authors who invite you to share their intimate knowledge and love of the areas covered.

Mull and Iona: Highways and Byways

Peter Macnab

ISBN 0 946487 58 8 PBK £4.95

 'The Isle of Mull is of Isles the fairest,
Of ocean's gems 'tis the first and rarest.'
So a local poet described it a hundred years ago, and this recently revised guide to Mull and sacred Iona, the most accessible islands of the Inner Hebrides, takes the reader on a delightful tour of these rare ocean gems, travelling with a native whose unparalleled knowledge and deep feeling for the area unlock the byways of the islands in all their natural beauty.

South West Scotland

Tom Atkinson

ISBN 0 946487 04 9 PBK £4.95

 This descriptive guide to the magical country of Robert Burns covers Kyle, Carrick, Galloway, Dumfriesshire, Kirkcudbrightshire and Wigtownshire. Hills, unknown moors and unspoiled beaches grace a land steeped in history and legend and portrayed with affection and deep delight.

An essential book for the visitor who yearns to feel at home in this land of peace and grandeur.

The West Highlands: The Lonely Lands

Tom Atkinson

ISBN 0 946487 56 1 PBK £4.95

 A guide to Inveraray, Glencoe, Loch Awe, Loch Lomond, Cowal, the Kyles of Bute and all of central Argyll written with insight, sympathy and loving detail. Once Atkinson has taken you there, these lands can never feel lonely.

'I have sought to make the complex simple, the beautiful accessible and the strange familiar,' he writes, and indeed he brings to the land a knowledge and affection only accessible to someone with intimate knowledge of the area.

A must for travellers and natives who want to delve beneath the surface.

'Highly personal and somewhat quirky... steeped in the lore of Scotland.'
THE WASHINGTON POST

The North West Highlands: Roads to the Isles

Tom Atkinson

ISBN 0 946487 54 5 PBK £4.95

 Ardnamurchan, Morvern, Morar, Moidart and the west coast to Ullapool are included in this guide to the Far West and Far North of Scotland. An unspoiled land of mountains, lochs and silver sands is brought to the walker's toe-tips (and to the reader's fingertips) in this stark, serene and evocative account of town, country and legend.

For any visitor to this Highland wonderland, Queen Victoria's favourite place on earth.

WALK WITH LUATH

Mountain Days & Bothy Nights

Dave Brown and Ian Mitchell

ISBN 0 946487 15 4 PBK £7.50

Acknowledged as a classic of mountain writing still in demand ten years after its first publication, this book takes you into the bothies, howffs and dosses on the Scottish hills. Fishgut Mac, Desperate Dan and Stumpy the Big Yin stalk hill and public house, evading gamekeepers and Royalty with a camaraderie which was the trademark of Scots hillwalking in the early days.

'The fun element comes through... how innocent the social polemic seems in our nastier world of today... the book for the rucksack this year.'
Hamish Brown, SCOTTISH MOUNTAINEERING CLUB JOURNAL

The Joy of Hillwalking

Ralph Storer

ISBN 0 946487 28 6 PBK £7.50

 Apart, perhaps, from the joy of sex, the joy of hillwalking brings more pleasure to more people than any other form of human activity.

'Alps, America, Scandinavia, you name it – Storer's been there, so why the hell shouldn't he bring all these various and varied places into his observations... [He] even admits to losing his virginity after a day on the Aggy Ridge... Well worth its place alongside Storer's earlier works.' TAC

Scotland's Mountains before the Mountaineers

Ian Mitchell

ISBN 0 946487 39 1 PBK £9.99

 In this ground-breaking book, Ian Mitchell tells the story of explorations and ascents in the Scottish Highlands in the days before mountaineering became a popular sport – when bandits, Jacobites, poachers and illicit distillers traditionally used the mountains as sanctuary. The book also gives a detailed account of the map makers, road builders, geologists, astronomers and naturalists, many of whom ascended hitherto untrodden summits while working in the Scottish Highlands.

Scotland's Mountains before the Mountaineers is divided into four Highland regions, with a map of each region showing key summits. While not designed primarily as a guide, it will be a useful handbook for walkers and climbers. Based on a wealth of new research, this book offers a fresh perspective that will fascinate climbers and mountaineers and everyone interested in the history of mountaineering, cartography, the evolution of landscape and the social history of the Scottish Highlands.

LUATH WALKING GUIDES

The highly respected and continually updated guides to the Cairngorms.

'Particularly good on local wildlife and how to see it' THE COUNTRYMAN

Walks in the Cairngorms

Ernest Cross
ISBN 0 946487 09 X PBK £4.95

This selection of walks celebrates the rare birds, animals, plants and geological wonders of a region often believed difficult to penetrate on foot. Nothing is difficult with this guide in your pocket, as Cross gives a choice for every walker, and includes valuable tips on mountain safety and weather advice.

Ideal for walkers of all ages and skiers waiting for snowier skies.

Short Walks in the Cairngorms

Ernest Cross
ISBN 0 946487 23 5 PBK £4.95

Cross wrote this volume after overhearing a walker remark that there were no short walks for lazy ramblers in the Cairngorm region. Here is the answer: rambles through scenic woods with a welcoming pub at the end, birdwatching hints, glacier holes, or for the fit and ambitious, scrambles up hills to admire vistas of glorious scenery. Wildlife in the Cairngorms is unequalled elsewhere in Britain, and here it is brought to the binoculars of any walker who treads quietly and with respect.

NATURAL SCOTLAND

Wild Scotland: The essential guide to finding the best of natural Scotland

James McCarthy
Photography by Laurie Campbell
ISBN 0 946487 37 5 PBK £7.50

With a foreword by Magnus Magnusson and striking colour photographs by Laurie Campbell, this is the essential up-to-date guide to viewing wildlife in Scotland for the visitor and resident alike. It provides a fascinating overview of the country's plants, animals, bird and marine life against the background of their typical natural settings, as an introduction to the vivid descriptions of the most accessible localities, linked to clear regional maps. A unique feature is the focus on 'green tourism' and sustainable visitor use of the countryside, contributed by Duncan Bryden, manager of the Scottish Tourist Board's Tourism and the Environment Task Force. Important practical information on access and the best times of year for viewing sites makes this an indispensable and user-friendly travelling companion to anyone interested in exploring Scotland's remarkable natural heritage.

James McCarthy is former Deputy Director for Scotland of the Nature Conservancy Council, and now a Board Member of Scottish Natural Heritage and Chairman of the Environmental Youth Work National Development Project Scotland.

'Nothing but Heather!'

Gerry Cambridge
ISBN 0 946487 49 9 PBK £15.00

Enter the world of Scottish nature – bizarre, brutal, often beautiful, always fascinating – as seen through the lens and poems of Gerry Cambridge, one of Scotland's most distinctive contemporary poets.

On film and in words, Cambridge brings unusual focus to bear on lives as diverse as those of dragonflies, hermit crabs, short-eared owls, and wood anemones. The result is both an instructive look by a naturalist at some of the flora and fauna of Scotland and a poet's aesthetic journey.

This exceptional collection comprises 48 poems matched with 48 captioned photographs. In his introduction Cambridge explores the origins of the project and the approaches to nature taken by other poets, and incorporates a wry account of an unwillingly-sectarian, farm-labouring, bird-obsessed adolescence in rural Ayrshire in the 1970s.

Keats felt that the beauty of a rainbow was somehow tarnished by knowledge of its properties. Yet the natural world is surely made more, not less, marvellous by awareness of its workings. In the poems that accompany these pictures, I have tried to give an inkling of that. May the marriage of verse and image enlarge the reader's appreciation and, perhaps, insight into the chomping, scurrying, quivering, procreating and dying kingdom, however many miles it be beyond the door.

GERRY CAMBRIDGE

'a real poet, with a sense of the music of language and the poetry of life...' KATHLEEN RAINE

'one of the most promising and original of modern Scottish poets... a master of form and subtlety.' GEORGE MACKAY BROWN

Scotland Land and People
An Inhabited Solitude

James McCarthy

ISBN 0 946487 57 X PBK £7.99

'Scotland is the country above all others that I have seen, in which a man of imagination may carve out his own pleasures; there are so many inhabited solitudes.'

DOROTH WORDSWORTH, in her journal of August 1803

An informed and thought-provoking profile of Scotland's unique landscapes and the impact of humans on what we see now and in the future. James McCarthy leads us through the many aspects of the land and the people who inhabit it: natural Scotland; the rocks beneath; land ownership; the use of resources; people and place; conserving Scotland's heritage and much more.

Written in a highly readable style, this concise volume offers an under-standing of the land as a whole. Emphasising the uniqueness of the Scottish environment, the author explores the links between this and other aspects of our culture as a key element in rediscovering a modern sense of the Scottish identity and perception of nationhood.

'This book provides an engaging introduction to the mysteries of Scotland's people and landscapes. Difficult concepts are described in simple terms, providing the interested Scot or tourist with an invaluable overview of the country... It fills an important niche which, to my knowledge, is filled by no other publications.'

BETSY KING, Chief Executive, Scottish Environmental Education Council.

The Highland Geology Trail

John L Roberts

ISBN 0946487 36 7 PBK £4.99

Where can you find the oldest rocks in Europe? Where can you see ancient hills around 800 million years old? How do you tell whether a valley was carved out by a glacier, not a river? What are the Fucoid Beds? Where do you find rocks folded like putty? How did great masses of rock pile up like snow in front of a snow-plough? When did volcanoes spew lava and ash to form Skye, Mull and Rum? Where can you find fossils on Skye?

'...a lucid introduction to the geological record in general, a jargon-free exposition of the regional background, and a series of descriptions of specific localities of geological interest on a "trail" around the highlands.

Having checked out the local references on the ground, I can vouch for their accuracy and look forward to investigating farther afield, informed by this guide.

Great care has been taken to explain specific terms as they occur and, in so doing, John Roberts has created a resource of great value which is eminently usable by anyone with an interest in the outdoors...the best bargain you are likely to get as a geology book in the foreseeable future.'

Jim Johnston, PRESS AND JOURNAL

Rum: Nature's Island

Magnus Magnusson

ISBN 0 946487 32 4   £7.95 PBK

Rum: Nature's Island is the fascinating story of a Hebridean island from the earliest times through to the Clearances and its period as the sporting playground of a Lancashire industrial magnate, and on to its rebirth as a National Nature Reserve, a model for the active ecological management of Scotland's wild places.

Thoroughly researched and written in a lively accessible style, the book includes comprehensive coverage of the island's geology, animals and plants, and people, with a special chapter on the Edwardian extravaganza of Kinloch Castle. There is practical information for visitors to what was once known as 'the Forbidden Isle'; the book provides details of bothy and other accommodation, walks and nature trails. It closes with a positive vision for the island's future: biologically diverse, economically dynamic and ecologically sustainable.

Rum: Nature's Island is published in co-operation with Scottish Natural Heritage (of which Magnus Magnusson is Chairman) to mark the 40th anniversary of the acquisition of Rum by its predecessor, The Nature Conservancy.

ON THE TRAIL OF

On the Trail of William Wallace

David R. Ross

ISBN 0 946487 47 2   PBK   £7.99

How close to reality was *Braveheart*?

Where was Wallace actually born?

What was the relationship between Wallace and Bruce?

Are there any surviving eye-witness accounts of Wallace?

How does Wallace influence the psyche of today's Scots?

On the Trail of William Wallace offers a refreshing insight into the life and heritage of the great Scots hero whose proud story is at the very heart of what it means to be Scottish. Not concentrating simply on the hard historical facts of Wallace's life, the book also takes into account the real significance of Wallace and his effect on the ordinary Scot through the ages, manifested in the many sites where his memory is marked.

In trying to piece together the jigsaw of the reality of Wallace's life, David Ross weaves a subtle flow of new information with his own observations. His engaging, thoughtful and at times amusing narrative reads with the ease of a historical novel, complete with all the intrigue, treachery and romance required to hold the attention of the casual reader and still entice the more knowledgable historian.

> 74 places to visit in Scotland and the north of England
> One general map and 3 location maps
> Stirling and Falkirk battle plans
> Wallace's route through London
> Chapter on Wallace connections in North America and elsewhere
> Reproductions of rarely seen illustrations

On the Trail of William Wallace will be enjoyed by anyone with an interest in Scotland, from the passing tourist to the most fervent nationalist. It is an encyclopaedia-cum-guide book, literally stuffed with fascinating titbits not usually on offer in the conventional history book.

David Ross is organiser of and historical adviser to the Society of William Wallace.

'Historians seem to think all there is to be known about Wallace has already been uncovered. Mr Ross has proved that Wallace studies are in fact in their infancy.' ELSPETH KING, Director the the Stirling Smith Art Museum & Gallery, who annotated and introduced the recent Luath edition of *Blind Harry's Wallace.*

'Better the pen than the sword!' RANDALL WALLACE, author of *Braveheart*, when asked by David Ross how it felt to be partly responsible for the freedom of a nation following the Devolution Referendum.

On the Trail of Robert the Bruce

David R. Ross

ISBN 0 946487 52 9   PBK   £7.99

On the Trail of Robert the Bruce charts the story of Scotland's hero-king from his boyhood, through his days of indecision as Scotland suffered under the English yoke, to his assumption of the crown exactly six months after the death of William Wallace. Here is the astonishing blow by blow

account of how, against fearful odds, Bruce led the Scots to win their greatest ever victory Bannockburn was not the end of the story. The war against English oppression lasted another fourteen years. Bruce lived just long enough to see his dreams of an independent Scotland come to fruition in 1328 with the signing of the Treaty of Edinburgh. The trail takes us to Bruce sites in Scotland, many of the little known and forgotten battle sites in northern England, and as far afield as the Bruce monuments in Andalusia and Jerusalem.

67 places to visit in Scotland and elsewhere.

One general map, 3 location maps and a map of Bruce-connected sites in Ireland.

Bannockburn battle plan.

Drawings and reproductions of rarely seen illustrations.

On the Trail of Robert the Bruce is not all blood and gore. It brings out the love and laughter, pain and passion of one of the great eras of Scottish history. Read it and you will understand why David Ross has never knowingly killed a spider in his life. Once again, he proves himself a master of the popular brand of hands-on history that made *On the Trail of William Wallace* so popular.

'*David R. Ross is a proud patriot and unashamed romantic.*'
SCOTLAND ON SUNDAY

'*Robert the Bruce knew Scotland, knew every class of her people, as no man who ruled her before or since has done. It was he who asked of her a miracle - and she accomplished it.*'
AGNES MUIR MACKENZIE

On the Trail of Robert Service

GW Lockhart
ISBN 0 946487 24 3 PBK £7.99

Robert Service is famed world-wide for his eye-witness verse-pictures of the Klondike goldrush. As a war poet, his work outsold Owen and Sassoon, and he went on to become the world's first million selling poet. In search of adventure and new experiences, he emigrated from Scotland to Canada in 1890 where he was caught up in the aftermath of the raging gold fever. His vivid dramatic verse bring to life the wild, larger than life characters of the gold rush Yukon, their bar-room brawls, their lust for

gold, their trigger-happy gambles with life and love. 'The Shooting of Dan McGrew' is perhaps his most famous poem:

A bunch of the boys were whooping it up in the Malamute saloon;
The kid that handles the music box was hitting a ragtime tune;
Back of the bar in a solo game, sat Dangerous Dan McGrew,
And watching his luck was his light o'love, the lady that's known as Lou.

His storytelling powers have brought Robert Service enduring fame, particularly in North America and Scotland where he is something of a cult figure.

Starting in Scotland, *On the Trail of Robert Service* follows Service as he wanders through British Columbia, Oregon, California, Mexico, Cuba, Tahiti, Russia, Turkey and the Balkans, finally 'settling' in France.

'*A fitting tribute to a remarkable man - a bank clerk who wanted to become a cowboy. It is hard to imagine a bank clerk writing such lines as:*

A bunch of boys were whooping it up...
The income from his writing actually exceeded his bank salary by a factor of five and he resigned to pursue a full time writing career.'
Charles Munn, THE SCOTTISH BANKER

'*Robert Service claimed he wrote for those who wouldnit be seen dead reading poetry. His was an almost unbelievably mobile life... Lockhart hangs on breathlessly, enthusiastically unearthing clues to the poet's life.*' Ruth Thomas, SCOTTISH BOOK COLLECTOR

'*This enthralling biography will delight Service lovers in both the Old World and the New.*' Marilyn Wright, SCOTS INDEPENDENT

On the Trail of Mary Queen of Scots

J. Keith Cheetham
ISBN 0 946487 50 2 PBK £7.99

Life dealt Mary Queen of Scots love, intrigue, betrayal and tragedy in generous measure.

On the Trail of Mary Queen of Scots traces the major events in the turbulent life of the beautiful, enigmatic queen whose romantic reign and tragic destiny exerts an undimmed fascination over 400 years after her execution.

Places of interest to visit – 99 in Scotland, 35 in England and 29 in France.

One general map and 6 location maps.

Line drawings and illustrations.

Simplified family tree of the royal houses of Tudor and Stuart.

Key sites include:

Linlithgow Palace - Mary's birthplace, now a magnificent ruin

Stirling Castle - where, only nine months old, Mary was crowned Queen of Scotland

Notre Dame Cathedral - where, aged fifteen, she married the future king of France

The Palace of Holyroodhouse - Rizzio, one of Mary's closest advisers, was murdered here and some say his blood still stains the spot where he was stabbed to death

Sheffield Castle - where for fourteen years she languished as prisoner of her cousin, Queen Elizabeth I

Fotheringhay - here Mary finally met her death on the executioner's block.

On the Trail of Mary Queen of Scots is for everyone interested in the life of perhaps the most romantic figure in Scotland's history; a thorough guide to places connected with Mary, it is also a guide to the complexities of her personal and public life.

'In my end is my beginning' MARY QUEEN OF SCOTS

'...the woman behaves like the Whore of Babylon' JOHN KNOX

MUSIC AND DANCE

Highland Balls and Village Halls

GW Lockhart

ISBN 0 946487 12 X PBK £6.95

Acknowledged as a classic in Scottish dancing circles throughout the world. Anecdotes, Scottish history, dress and dance steps are all included in this *'delightful little book, full of interest... both a personal account and an understanding look at the making of traditions.'* NEW ZEALAND SCOTTISH COUNTRY DANCES MAGAZINE

'A delightful survey of Scottish dancing and custom. Informative, concise and opinionated, it guides the reader across the history and geography of country dance and ends by detailing the 12 dances every Scot should know – the most famous being the Eightsome Reel, "the greatest longest, rowdiest, most diabolically executed of all the Scottish country dances" .' THE HERALD

'A pot-pourri of every facet of Scottish country dancing. It will bring back memories of petronella turns and poussettes and make you eager to take part in a Broun's reel or a dashing white sergeant!' DUNDEE COURIER AND ADVERTISER

'An excellent an very readable insight into the traditions and customs of Scottish country dancing. The author takes us on a tour from his own early days jigging in the village hall to the characters and traditions that have made our own brand of dance popular throughout the world.' SUNDAY POST

Fiddles & Folk: A celebration of the re-emergence of Scotland's musical heritage

GW Lockhart

ISBN 0 946487 38 3 PBK £7.95

In *Fiddles & Folk*, his companion volume to *Highland Balls and Village Halls*, Wallace Lockhart meets up with many of the people who have created the renaissance of Scot-land's music at home and overseas.

From Dougie MacLean, Hamish Henderson, the Battlefield Band, the Whistlebinkies, the Scottish Fiddle Orchestra, the McCalmans and many more come the stories that break down the musical barriers between Scotland's past and present, and between the diverse musical forms which have woven together to create the dynamism of the music today.

'I have tried to avoid a formal approach to Scottish music as it affects those of us with our musical heritage coursing through our veins. The picture I have sought is one of many brush strokes, looking at how some individuals have come to the fore, examining their music, lives, thoughts, even philosophies...' WALLACE LOCKHART

'"I never had a narrow, woolly-jumper, fingers stuck in the ear approach to music. We have a musical heritage here that is the envy of the rest of the world. Most countries just can't compete," he [Ian Green, Greentrax] says. And as young Scots tire of Oasis and Blur, they will realise that there is a wealth of young Scottish music on their doorstep just waiting to be discovered.' THE SCOTSMAN

For anyone whose heart lifts at the sound of fiddle or pipes, this book takes you on a delightful journey, full of humour and respect, in the company of some of the performers who have taken Scotland's music around the world and come back enriched.

LUATH GRAPHICS

Old Scotland New Scotland

Jeff Fallow

ISBN 0 946487 40 5 PBK £6.99

'Together we can build a new Scotland based on Labour's values.' DONALD DEWAR, Party Political Broadcast

'Despite the efforts of decent Mr Dewar, the voters may yet conclude they are looking at the same old hacks in brand new suits.' IAN BELL, *The Independent*

'At times like this you suddenly realise how dangerous the neglect of Scottish history in our schools and universities may turn out to be.' MICHAEL FRY, *The Herald*

'...one of the things I hope will go is our chip on the shoulder about the English... The SNP has a huge responsibility to articulate Scottish independence in a way that is pro-Scottish and not anti-English.' ALEX SALMOND, *The Scotsman*

Scottish politics have never been more exciting. In *old Scotland new Scotland* Jeff Fallow takes us on a graphic voyage through Scotland's turbulent history, from earliest times through to the present day and beyond. This fast-track guide is the quick way to learn what your history teacher didn't tell you, essential reading for all who seek an understanding of Scotland and its history. Eschewing the romanticisation of his country's past, Fallow offers a new perspective on an old nation. 'Too many people associate Scottish history with tartan trivia or outworn romantic myth. This book aims to blast that stubborn idea.' JEFF FALLOW

BIOGRAPHY

Tobermory Teuchter: A first-hand account of life on Mull in the early years of the 20th century

Peter Macnab

ISBN 0 946487 41 3 PBK £7.99

Peter Macnab was reared on Mull, as was his father, and his grandfather before him. In this book he provides a revealing account of life on Mull during the first quarter of the 20th century, focusing especially on the years of World War I. This enthralling social history of the island is set against Peter Macnab's early years as son of the governor of the Mull Poorhouse, one of the last in the Hebrides, and is illustrated throughout by photographs from his exceptional collec-tion. Peter Macnab's 'fisherman's yarns' and other personal reminis-cences are told delightfully by a born storyteller.

This latest work from the author of a range of books about the island, including the standard study of Mull and Iona, reveals his unparalleled knowledge of and deep feeling for Mull and its people. After his long career with the Clydesdale Bank, first in Tobermory and later on the mainland, Peter, now 94, remains a teuchter at heart, proud of his island heritage.

'Peter Macnab is a man of words who doesn't mince his words - not where his beloved Mull is concerned. 'I will never forget some of the inmates of the poorhouse,' says Peter. 'Some of them were actually victims of the later Clearances. It was history at first hand, and there was no romance about it'. But Peter Macnab sees little creative point in crying over ancient injustices. For him the task is to help Mull in this century and beyond.'
SCOTS MAGAZINE, May 1998

Bare Feet and Tackety Boots

Archie Cameron

ISBN 0 946487 17 0 PBK £7.95

The island of Rum before the First World War was the playground of its rich absentee landowner. A survivor of life a century gone tells his story. Factors and schoolmasters, midges and poaching, deer, ducks and MacBrayne's steamers: here social history and personal anecdote create a record of a way of life gone not long ago but already almost forgotten. This is the story the gentry couldn't tell.

'This book is an important piece of social history, for it gives an insight into how the other half lived in an era the likes of which will never be seen again' FORTHRIGHT MAGAZINE

'The authentic breath of the pawky, country-wise estate employee.'
THE OBSERVER

'Well observed and detailed account of island life in the early years of this century'. THE SCOTS MAGAZINE

'A very good read with the capacity to make the reader chuckle. A very talented writer.'
STORNOWAY GAZETTE

Come Dungeons Dark

John Taylor Caldwell

ISBN 0 946487 19 7   PBK   £6.95

Glasgow anarchist Guy Aldred died with 10p in his pocket in 1963 claiming there was better company in Barlinnie Prison than in the Corridors of Power. 'The Red Scourge' is remembered here by one who worked with him and spent 27 years as part of his turbulent household, sparring with Lenin, Sylvia Pankhurst and others as he struggled for freedom for his beloved fellow-man.

'The welcome and long-awaited biography of... one of this country's most prolific radical propagandists... Crank or visionary?... whatever the verdict, the Glasgow anarchist has finally been given a fitting memorial.' THE SCOTSMAN

FICTION

The Bannockburn Years

William Scott

ISBN 0 946487 34 0   PBK   £7.95

A present day Edinburgh solicitor stumbles across reference to a document of value to the Nation State of Scotland. He tracks down the document on the Isle of Bute, a document which probes the real 'quaestiones' about nationhood and national identity. The document ends up being published, but is it authentic and does it matter? Almost 700 years on, these 'quaestiones' are still worth asking.

Written with pace and passion, William Scott has devised an intriguing vehicle to open up new ways of looking at the future of Scotland and its people. He presents an alternative interpretation of how the Battle of Bannockburn was fought, and through the Bannatyne manuscript he draws the reader into the minds of those involved. Winner of the 1997 Constable Trophy, the premier award in Scotland for an unpublished novel, this book offers new insights to both the academic and the general reader which are sure to provoke further discussion and debate.

'A brilliant storyteller. I shall expect to see your name writ large hereafter.' NIGEL TRANTER, October 1997.

'... a compulsive read.' PH Scott, THE SCOTSMAN

The Great Melnikov

Hugh MacLachlan

ISBN 0 946487 42 1   PBK £7.95

A well crafted, gripping novel, written in a style reminiscent of John Buchan and set in London and the Scottish Highlands during the First World War, The Great Melnikov is a dark tale of double-cross and deception. We first meet Melnikov, one-time star of the German circus, languishing as a down-and-out in Trafalgar Square. He soon finds himself drawn into a tortuous web of intrigue. He is a complex man whose personal struggle with alcoholism is an inner drama which parallels the tense twists and turns as a spy mystery unfolds. Melnikov's options are narrowing. The circle of threat is closing. Will Melnikov outwit the sinister enemy spy network? Can he summon the will and the wit to survive?

Hugh MacLachlan, in his first full length novel, demonstrates an undoubted ability to tell a good story well. His earlier stories have been broadcast on Radio Scotland, and he has the rare distinction of being shortlisted for the Macallan/Scotland on Sunday Short Story Competition two years in succession.

FOLKLORE

The Supernatural Highlands

Francis Thompson

ISBN 0 946487 31 6   PBK   £8.99

An authoritative exploration of the otherworld of the Highlander, happenings and beings hitherto thought to be outwith the ordinary forces of nature. A simple introduction to the way of life of rural Highland and Island communities, this new edition weaves a path through second sight, the evil eye, witchcraft, ghosts, fairies and other supernatural beings, offering new sight-lines on areas of belief once dismissed as folklore and superstition.

Tall Tales from an Island

Peter Macnab

ISBN 0 946487 07 3   PBK   £8.99

Peter Macnab was born and reared on Mull. He heard many of these tales as a lad, and others he has listened to in later years.

There are humorous tales, grim tales, witty tales, tales of witchcraft, tales of love, tales of heroism, tales of treachery, historical tales and tales of yesteryear.

A popular lecturer, broadcaster and writer, Peter Macnab is the author of a number of books and articles about Mull, the island he knows so intimately and loves so much. As he himself puts it in his introduction to this book 'I am of the unswerving opinion that nowhere else in the world will you find a better way of life, nor a finer people with whom to share it.'

'All islands, it seems, have a rich store of characters whose stories represent a kind of subculture without which island life would be that much poorer. Macnab has succeeded in giving the retelling of the stories a special Mull flavour, so much so that one can visualise the storytellers sitting on a bench outside the house with a few cronies, puffing on their pipes and listening with nodding approval.' WEST HIGHLAND FREE PRESS

SPORT

Over the Top with the Tartan Army (Active Service 1992-97)

Andrew McArthur

ISBN 0 946487 45 6 PBK £7.99

Scotland has witnessed the growth of a new and curious military phenomenon – grown men bedecked in tartan yomping across the globe, hellbent on benevolence and ritualistic bevvying. What noble cause does this famous army serve? Why, football of course!

Taking us on an erratic world tour, McArthur gives a frighteningly funny insider's eye view of active service with the Tartan Army - the madcap antics of Scotland's travelling support in the '90s, written from the inside, covering campaigns and skirmishes from Euro '92 up to the qualifying drama for France '98 in places as diverse as Russia, the Faroes, Belarus, Sweden, Monte Carlo, Estonia, Latvia, USA and Finland.

This book is a must for any football fan who likes a good laugh.

'I commend this book to all football supporters'. Graham Spiers, SCOTLAND ON SUNDAY

'In wishing Andy McArthur all the best with this publication, I do hope he will be in a position to produce a sequel after our participation in the World Cup in France'. CRAIG BROWN, Scotland Team Coach

All royalties on sales of the book are going to Scottish charities.

Ski & Snowboard Scotland

Hilary Parke

ISBN 0 946487 35 9 PBK £6.99

Snowsports in Scotland are still a secret treasure. There's no need to go abroad when there's such an exciting variety of terrain right here on your doorstep. You just need to know what to look for. *Ski & Snowboard Scotland* is aimed at maximising the time you have available so that the hours you spend on the snow are memorable for all the right reasons.

This fun and informative book guides you over the slopes of Scotland, giving you the inside track on all the major ski centres. There are chapters ranging from how to get there to the impact of snowsports on the environment.

'Reading the book brought back many happy memories of my early training days at the dry slope in Edinburgh and of many brilliant weekends in the Cairngorms.' EMMA CARRICK-ANDERSON, from her foreword, written in the US, during a break in training for her first World Cup as a member of the British Alpine Ski Team.

SOCIAL HISTORY

Notes from the North incorporating a Brief History of the Scots and the English

Emma Wood

ISBN 0 946487 46 4 PBK £8.99

Notes on being English
Notes on being in Scotland
Learning from a shared past

Sickened by the English jingoism that surfaced

in rampant form during the 1982 Falklands War, Emma Wood started to dream of moving from her home in East Anglia to the Highlands of Scotland. She felt increasingly frustrated and marginalised as Thatcherism got a grip on the southern English psyche. The Scots she met on frequent holidays in the Highlands had no truck with Thatcherism, and she felt at home with grassroots Scottish anti-authoritarianism. The decision was made. She uprooted and headed for a new life in the north of Scotland.

'An intelligent and perceptive book... calm, reflective, witty and sensitive. It should certainly be read by all English visitors to Scotland, be they tourists or incomers. And it should certainly be read by all Scots concerned about what kind of nation we live in. They might learn something about themselves.'
THE HERALD

'... her enlightenment is evident on every page of this perceptive, provocative book.'
MAIL ON SUNDAY

A Word for Scotland

Jack Campbell
with a foreword by Magnus Magnusson
ISBN 0 946487 48 0 PBK £12.99

'A word for Scotland' was Lord Beaverbrook's hope when he founded the *Scottish Daily Express*. That word for Scotland quickly became, and was for many years, the national newspaper of Scotland.

The pages of *A Word For Scotland* exude warmth and a wry sense of humour. Jack Campbell takes us behind the scenes to meet the larger-than-life characters and ordinary people who made and recorded the stories. Here we hear the stories behind the stories that hit the headlines in this great yarn of journalism in action.

It would be true to say 'all life is here'. From the Cheapside Street fire of which cost the lives of 19 Glasgow firemen, to the theft of the Stone of Destiny, to the lurid exploits of serial killer Peter Manuel, to encounters with world boxing champions Benny Lynch and Cassius Clay - this book offers telling glimpses of the characters, events, joy and tragedy which make up Scotland's story in the 20th century.

'As a rookie reporter you were proud to work on it and proud to be part of it - it was fine newspaper right at the heartbeat of Scotland.'
RONALD NEIL, Chief Executive of BBC Production, and a reporter on the *Scottish Daily Express* (1963-68)

'This book is a fascinating reminder of Scottish journalism in its heyday. It will be read avidly by those journalists who take pride in their profession – and should be compulsory reading for those who don't.'
JACK WEBSTER, columnist on *The Herald* and *Scottish Daily Express* journalist (1960-80)

The Crofting Years

Francis Thompson
ISBN 0 946487 06 5 PBK £6.95

Crofting is much more than a way of life. It is a storehouse of cultural, linguistic and moral values which holds together a scattered and struggling rural population. This book fills a blank in the written history of crofting over the last two centuries. Bloody conflicts and gunboat diplomacy, treachery, compassion, music and story: all figure in this mine of information on crofting in the Highlands and Islands of Scotland.

'I would recommend this book to all who are interested in the past, but even more so to those who are interested in the future survival of our way of life and culture'
STORNOWAY GAZETTE

'The book is a mine of information on many aspects of the past, among them the homes, the food, the music and the medicine of our crofting forebears.'
John M Macmillan, erstwhile CROFTERS COMMISSIONER FOR LEWIS AND HARRIS

POETRY

Blind Harry's Wallace

William Hamilton of Gilbertfield
Introduced by Elspeth King
ISBN 0 946487 43 X HBK £15.00
ISBN 0 946487 33 2 PBK £8.99

The original story of the real braveheart, Sir William Wallace. Racy, blood on every page, violently anglo-phobic, grossly embellished, vulgar and disgus-ting, clumsy and stilted, a literary failure, a great epic.

Whatever the verdict on BLIND HARRY, this is the book which has done more than any other to frame the notion of Scotland's national identity. Despite its numerous 'historical inaccuracies', it remains the principal source for what we now know about the life of Wallace.

The novel and film *Braveheart* were based on the 1722 Hamilton edition of this epic poem. Burns, Wordsworth, Byron and others were greatly influenced by this version 'wherein the old obsolete words are rendered more intelligible', which is said to be the book, next to the Bible, most commonly found in Scottish households in the eighteenth century. Burns even admits to having 'borrowed... a couplet worthy of Homer' directly from Hamilton's version of BLIND HARRY to include in 'Scots wha hae'.

Elspeth King, in her introduction to this, the first accessible edition of BLIND HARRY in verse form since 1859, draws parallels between the situation in Scotland at the time of Wallace and that in Bosnia and Chechnya in the 1990s. Seven hundred years to the day after the Battle of Stirling Bridge, the 'Settled Will of the Scottish People' was expressed in the devolution referendum of 11 September 1997. She describes this as a landmark opportunity for mature reflection on how the nation has been shaped, and sees BLIND HARRY'S WALLACE as an essential and compelling text for this purpose.

'A true bard of the people'.
TOM SCOTT, THE PENGUIN BOOK OF SCOTTISH VERSE, on Blind Harry.

'A more inventive writer than Shakespeare'.
RANDALL WALLACE

'The story of Wallace poured a Scottish prejudice in my veins which will boil along until the floodgates of life shut in eternal rest'.
ROBERT BURNS

'Hamilton's couplets are not the best poetry you will ever read, but they rattle along at a fair pace. In re-issuing this work, the publishers have re-opened the spring from which most of our conceptions of the Wallace legend come'.
SCOTLAND ON SUNDAY

'The return of Blind Harry's Wallace, a man who makes Mel look like a wimp'.
THE SCOTSMAN

Poems to be read aloud

Collected and with an introduction by Tom Atkinson
ISBN 0 946487 00 6 PBK £5.00

This personal col-lection of doggerel and verse ranging from the tear-jerking *Green Eye of the Yellow God* to the rarely printed, bawdy *Eskimo Nell* has a lively cult following. Much borrowed and rarely returned, this is a book for reading aloud in very good company, preferably after a dram or twa. You are guaranteed a warm welcome if you arrive at a gathering with this little volume in your pocket.

'This little book is an attempt to stem the great rushing tide of canned entertainment. A hopeless attempt of course. There is poetry of very high order here, but there is also some fearful doggerel. But that is the way of things. No literary axe is being ground.

Of course some of the items in this book are poetic drivel, if read as poems. But that is not the point. They all spring to life when they are read aloud. It is the combination of the poem with your voice, with all the art and craft you can muster, that produces the finished product and effect you seek.

You don't have to learn the poems. Why clutter up your mind with rubbish? Of course, it is a poorly furnished mind that doesn't carry a fair stock of poetry, but surely the poems to be remembered and savoured in secret, when in love, or ill, or sad, are not the ones you want to share with an audience.

So go ahead, clear your throat and transfix all talkers with a stern eye, then let rip!'
TOM ATKINSON

Luath Press Limited
committed to publishing well written books worth reading

LUATH PRESS takes its name from Robert Burns, whose little collie Luath (*Gael.*, swift or nimble) tripped up Jean Armour at a wedding and gave him the chance to speak to the woman who was to be his wife and the abiding love of his life. Burns called one of *The Twa Dogs* Luath after Cuchullin's hunting dog in *Ossian's Fingal*. Luath Press grew up in the heart of Burns country, and now resides a few steps up the road from Burns' first lodgings in Edinburgh's Royal Mile.

Luath offers you distinctive writing with a hint of unexpected pleasures.

Most UK bookshops either carry our books in stock or can order them for you. To order direct from us, please send a £sterling cheque, postal order, international money order or your credit card details (number, address of cardholder and expiry date) to us at the address below. Please add post and packing as follows: UK – £1.00 per delivery address; overseas surface mail – £2.50 per delivery address; overseas airmail – £3.50 for the first book to each delivery address, plus £1.00 for each additional book by airmail to the same address. If your order is a gift, we will happily enclose your card or message at no extra charge.

Luath Press Limited
543/2 Castlehill
The Royal Mile
Edinburgh EH1 2ND
Telephone: 0131 225 4326 (24 hours)
Fax: 0131 225 4324
email: gavin.macdougall@luath.co.uk
Website: www.luath.co.uk